National Park Trips Media

ROAD TRIP
YELLOWSTONE

ADVENTURES JUST OUTSIDE
AMERICA'S FAVORITE PARK

DINA MISHEV

Guilford, Connecticut

National Park Trips Media's mission is to inspire travelers through authentic storytelling to take a great American road trip to a national park. It is part of Active Interest Media's Outdoor Group.

An imprint of Globe Pequot

Distributed by NATIONAL BOOK NETWORK

Copyright © 2018 by ACTIVE INTEREST MEDIA

British Library Cataloguing in Publication Information Available

Library of Congress Cataloging-in-Publication Data

Names: Mishev, Dina, author.
Title: Road trip Yellowstone : adventures just outside America's favorite park / Dina Mishev.
Description: Guilford, Connecticut : Lyons Press, 2018. | Includes index.
Identifiers: LCCN 2017048250 | ISBN 9781493030309 (pbk.) ISBN 9781493030316 [e-book]
Subjects: LCSH: Yellowstone National Park Region–Description and travel.
Classification: LCC F722 .M57 2018 | DDC 917.87/520434–dc23 LC record available at https://lccn.loc.gov/2017048250

∞™ The paper used in this publication meets the minimum requirements of American National Standard
for Information Sciences–Permanence of Paper for Printed Library Materials, ANSI/NISO Z39.48-1992.

Printed in the United States of America

CONTENTS

N

MONTANA

Yellowstone River

94

BILLINGS

0 10 20 40
MILES

310

CROW RESERVATION

NORTHERN
CHEYENNE
INDIAN
RESERVATION

90

BIGHORN
CANYON
NATIONAL
RECREATION
AREA

art
untain
erpretive
ter

ALT
14

Pryor
Mountain
Wild Mustang
Center

14

310

14

90

14

16

WYOMING

20

20

16

16

16

90

ETEETSE

120

Legend Rocks
State Petroglyph Site

16

20

25

Hot Springs
State Park

CASPER, CHEYENNE,
& FORT COLLINS, COLORADO

THERMOPOLIS

Wyoming Dinosaur Center

DOLLY HOLMES

INTRODUCTION

My first trip to Yellowstone was the summer before I started eighth grade. We hit it on a family road trip west from our home in Maryland. I'd like to say my memories of those days were vivid and exciting. I'd be lying. For weeks before we left home, my dad, who had lived in Great Falls, Montana, and spent many weekends exploring Yellowstone in the 1960s before marrying my mom, told my younger brother and I stories about bears that stuck their heads into your car, even your tent. There were tales about water exploding up out of seemingly nowhere. I couldn't wait to experience these things myself.

By the time my family made it to Yellowstone in the late 1980s, the park had begun managing human/bear interactions. And by "managing," they meant preventing them from happening as much as possible. We didn't see a single bear in the park, much less have one stick its head into our tent.

To a precociously imaginative kid like myself, tales about water exploding suddenly out of the ground had conjured up a vision much more awesome than the reality of Old Faithful. (Nothing less than a Mt. St. Helens–level eruption would have satisfied my expectations.) Since I knew little to nothing about geology, I couldn't appreciate the awesomeness happening underground that caused Old Faithful's faithfulness.

But the trip wasn't totally a waste. I do have vivid memories of driving around Jackson, Wyoming, looking for a hotel when we rolled into town without a reservation (some things don't change). I remember our car muscling its way up the Beartooth Pass between Cooke City and Red Lodge, Montana, and thinking it improbable and astonishing that such a landscape, and road, existed. How had a road been built in such hostile geology? There were snowbanks, taller even than my mom and dad! I could have a snowball fight with my younger brother! In August! How could this many lakes exist so close to each other, and each be more beautiful than the last? And there was the bear I so wanted to see, even if it was a speck in the distance (and might really have been a tree stump). My takeaway from that trip was that Yellowstone was so much more than the national park. The whole area around the park was magic.

Immediately after graduating from college, I ended up moving to Jackson, an hour from Yellowstone's South Entrance. But, for more than 20 years now, I've been working on appreciating the awesomeness of the world's first national park, and having experiences in it not even my prolifically creative 12-year-old self could have thought up.

Exploring Yellowstone has brought me much joy, but exploring the towns and communities around it has brought me even more. Since there is no shortage of books about Yellowstone, the world's first national park, this book focuses instead on the communities around the park. Yellowstone is unique among America's 143 national parks and monuments for many reasons, including the fact it has five different entrances, each of which is at least a 2-hour drive from its nearest neighboring entrance. Yellowstone is larger in size than Rhode Island, Delaware, and Washington, DC, combined.

The communities nearest these five entrances—Jackson Hole and Cody, Wyoming, and West Yellowstone, Cooke City, and Gardiner, Montana—are as diverse as the geological wonders within Yellowstone. This book starts at each of Yellowstone's gateway communities and then, extending about 100 miles away from the park, tells the stories of people, events, local institutions, and places in an attempt to provide a true and well-rounded sense of place.

Within 100 miles of a Yellowstone entrance, you'll find everything from the seed potato capital of the world to the country's second-largest Superfund site, the continent's most challenging ski resort, an artist who majored in agricultural business, the largest National Historic District in the country, a wildlife art museum that includes pieces by Picasso and Warhol in its collection, and a bakery that makes the best *pain au chocolat* this side of Paris, among other things. Most of the road trips are organized geographically—keeping the people, places, and events of Teton Valley, Idaho, or of Butte, Montana, together. But every once in a while—like with the art and culture scene in Jackson Hole near the southern entrance—I made a road trip thematic.

I gave up a winter of skiing to write this book. If you enjoy reading it half as much as I enjoyed researching and writing it, I'll consider the sacrifice worth it.

THE ENTRANCES

Located mainly in northwestern Wyoming, Yellowstone National Park is the world's first national park. Parts of it also stretch into Idaho and Montana. To access the park, choose between five entrances and their nearby towns.

NORTHEAST ENTRANCE

Closest to Cooke City, Montana, and its sister village Silver Gate, Montana, this entrance gives you the best access to Yellowstone's legendary Lamar Valley where grizzlies, black bears, bison, and wolves roam. Tucked between Yellowstone's Northeast Entrance and the imposing Beartooth Mountains, the tiny outpost of Cooke City (year-round population: seventy-five) has a downtown that spans only a few blocks but offers good dining and lodging options. In summer, travelers can reach Cooke City via the Beartooth Highway or the park. In winter, this entrance is closed and the only way into the park is through Yellowstone's North Entrance near Gardiner.

NORTH ENTRANCE

Want to experience some of the West's most spectacular scenery in a town that can feel like a cross between *Northern Exposure* and Animal Planet, given its wild neighbors living up the street in Yellowstone National Park? Head to Gardiner, Montana, just 5 miles from the steaming terraces of Yellowstone's Mammoth Hot Springs, one of the park's many natural wonders. Sitting at the only year-round entrance to the world's first national park, pretty much everything in Gardiner is colorful from the scenery and people to the names of dishes on menus, adding a poetic slant to your visit.

NICK COTE

EAST ENTRANCE

The closest town to Yellowstone's East Entrance is 50 miles away in Cody, Wyoming. Named after onetime resident and western showman Buffalo Bill Cody, it's home to a top-notch museum complex, an Old West replica town, and historic reenactments. Cody doesn't disappoint on the modern front either. There are lively rodeos, down-home restaurants, and even a zipline. The closest year-round airport to Yellowstone National Park (Yellowstone Regional Airport) is here, making Cody an especially convenient launching point for trips to the park.

SOUTH ENTRANCE

Take one part historic cowboy charm, add a healthy dash of modern glamour, and finish with a heaping portion of world-class mountain scenery, and you've got Jackson, Wyoming—Yellowstone's southern gateway town and one of the most beloved getaways in the Rocky Mountains. Situated on the doorstep of Grand Teton National Park (GTNP) and 57 miles from Yellowstone's South Entrance, Jackson's (Jackson Hole refers to the entire valley) fantastic dining, outdoor recreation, and cultural attractions make it more than worth a visit in its own right. This entrance is convenient for those wanting to visit Grand Teton National Park in addition to Yellowstone. It's home to the Jackson Hole Airport, which is serviced by a handful of airlines.

WEST ENTRANCE

This entrance is the park's busiest, so it's no wonder that West Yellowstone, Montana, is a bustling gateway with dining, shopping, and attractions for travelers. Located just across the Wyoming border in Montana, West Yellowstone is a convenient entrance town for those coming from Idaho or western Montana, especially Missoula. Visitors will find lots of Wild West flavor, plenty of lodging, and a mix of cultural and outdoor activities. Catch a show at the Playmill Theatre or study up for your park trip at Yellowstone IMAX, which shows a rotating series of movies about Yellowstone, wildlife, and pioneer history.

WHERE TO STAY

With nine accommodation options in Yellowstone National Park, it can be difficult to figure out where you should stay in the summer. Do you stay in a historic hotel near Old Faithful or a cabin closer to the wildlife lounging in the Lamar Valley? Read on to find the lodging that best suits your needs. Be forewarned that there are no TVs, radios, or air-conditioning in park accommodations, but the fresh night air will cool you down enough to want a blanket. If you are planning on visiting in winter, there are only two lodges open in the park: Mammoth Hot Springs Hotel & Cabins and Old Faithful Snow Lodge & Cabins.

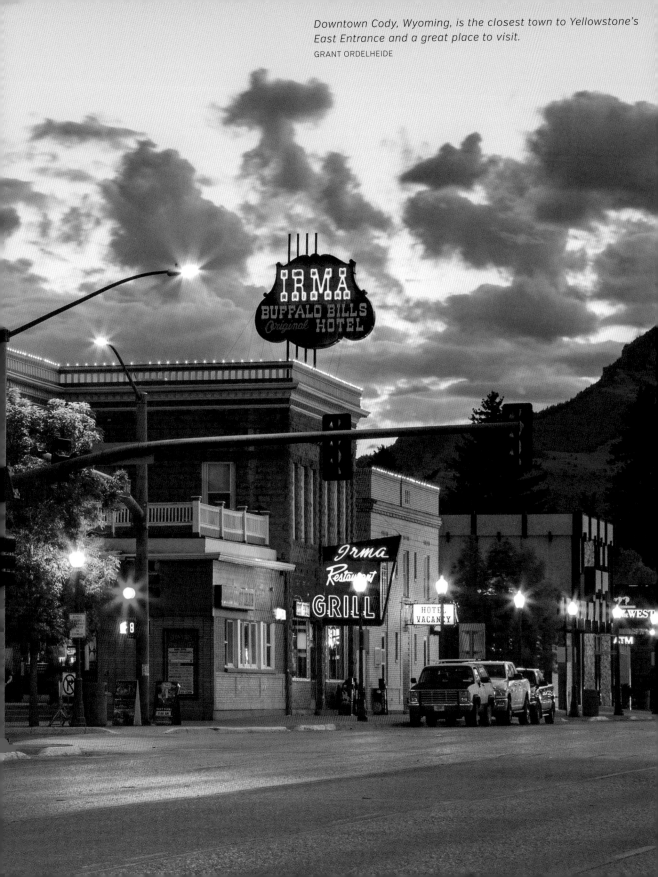

↑ OLD FAITHFUL INN

Built in the early 1900s, the Old Faithful Inn is arguably Yellowstone's most iconic hotel. It's certainly the hotel that garners the most reservation requests every year. It's a National Historic Landmark and the world's largest log cabin structure. Its lobby was designed to create a sense of community, and you will literally find people from all over the world gathering here, swapping stories and listening to the live piano music. The inn has 327 rooms, ranging from suites and luxury rooms to rooms without bathrooms. It typically opens in early May and closes in early October.

OLD FAITHFUL LODGE CABINS

Not to be confused with its older neighbor, the Old Faithful Inn, the Old Faithful Lodge Cabins offer great views of the iconic Old Faithful geyser. There are log cabins that were built during the 1920s in addition to a one-story lodge with large logs, stone pillars, and a cafeteria-style food court. In 2016, sixty-seven cabins were renovated to provide guests with a more contemporary cabin experience. The cabins are typically open mid-May to early October.

MAMMOTH HOT SPRINGS HOTEL & CABINS

Stay at Mammoth Hot Springs Hotel & Cabins and you'll be within a few minutes' walk of Mammoth Hot Springs, the peculiar terraced hot springs you can explore via boardwalk. Located near the North Entrance of the park near Gardiner, Montana, and built in 1936, this grand hotel and cabins offers rooms or cabins with or without bathrooms and a cabin that features a six-person outdoor hot tub. It also features a guest wing that was originally built in 1911. In 2017, the hotel lobby, retail shop, map room, and hotel rooms were renovated. During the summer season, it's open late April through early October. In winter, it's open mid-December through early March.

ROOSEVELT LODGE CABINS

At Roosevelt Lodge Cabins, you are a short drive from the wildlife mecca of Yellowstone's grand Lamar Valley. Choose between two types of cabins to spend the night. The Frontier Cabins have two double beds and are equipped with a shower, toilet, and sink. The Roughrider Cabins are a bit more spartan. Each comes with one or two double beds and a wood-burning stove to keep you warm. There are no bathrooms in these cabins, but you can use a communal shower and bathroom facility nearby.

All cabins are a short stroll to Roosevelt Lodge, one of the most charming and intimate restaurants in the park. Just to be clear, the lodge itself is a restaurant, not a hotel. The cabins typically open in early June and close early September.

Next page: If you're visiting Mammoth Hot Springs, you can stay at Mammoth Hot Springs Hotel & Cabins.
JIM PEACO/NATIONAL PARK SERVICE

GRANT ORDELHEIDE

LAKE YELLOWSTONE HOTEL & CABINS

While many think Old Faithful Inn is the oldest in the park, they are incorrect. Built in 1891, Lake Yellowstone Hotel & Cabins wins the prize. Located near the shores of Yellowstone Lake and Hayden Valley, which is known for its wildlife, this beautiful yellow hotel with large white columns underwent a $28.5 million renovation in 2014. The renovation included all guest rooms, the dining room, bar, and public spaces and a redesigned deli. Lake Yellowstone Hotel offers wired Internet service and a business center. Choose among suites, deluxe hotel rooms, standard rooms, and even cabins clustered near the hotel. The hotel opens mid-May and closes early October.

LAKE LODGE CABINS

Located near the shores of Yellowstone Lake, the Lake Lodge Cabins' lodge is a charming shingle and log-hewn building with a large porch. Inside are two fireplaces. Choose among 186 cabins, many built in the 1920s, and some built later, that come with a variety of amenities. The Western Cabins are the priciest and are built in modules of four or six and are furnished with two queen beds. The Frontier Cabins were built in the 1920s but recently renovated and feature one or two double beds and a bathroom. The Pioneer Cabins are the least expensive and were built in the 1920s. They feature one or two double beds and a bathroom. The cabins are open early to mid-June to late September.

OLD FAITHFUL SNOW LODGE & CABINS

Built in 1999, this lodge is the newest kid in the park, the latest full-service lodge to spring up in Yellowstone. It's near the legendary Old Faithful Geyser and offers a full-service dining room, quick-service Geyser Grill, and a gift store. It's tucked a little farther away from the action in comparison to its sister hotels, the Old Faithful Inn and Old Faithful Lodge Cabins. Because it's less than 20 years old, its appearance, furnishings, and decor are contemporary. Choose between two types of lodge rooms or two types of cabins. For the summer season, the lodge opens at the end of April and closes at the end of October. In winter, the lodge opens mid-December and closes early March.

GRANT ORDELHEIDE

GRANT VILLAGE

Closest to Grand Teton National Park, which lies south of Yellowstone, Grant Village was built in 1984 and is in the West Thumb area of Yellowstone. It has six two-story lodges with fifty rooms each. The lodge rooms were remodeled in spring 2015 and include two double beds, a bathroom with a shower or shower/bath combination, and an activity table with chairs. You can keep small items cool in the room refrigerator and satisfy your caffeine fix with the coffee brewer. There's the Lake House Restaurant with large windows looking right out onto the lake. Or dine in the pines at the Grant Village Dining Room, a full-service restaurant that sits amid lodgepole pine trees and offers views of the lake. Grant Village lodging accommodations are open mid-May through early October.

CANYON LODGE & CABINS

Located on the park's east side near the Grand Canyon of the Yellowstone River, the Canyon Lodge & Cabins is the biggest lodging property in Yellowstone. It also underwent a 2-year lodging redevelopment that included the construction of five new lodges and 400 guest rooms. Choose among a variety of suites, lodge rooms, and cabins. Since its renovation, the property is now hailed as a very eco-friendly place to stay. When you walk in, you'll find wainscoting and coat racks made from beetle-kill wood, which is wood from pine trees in the region decimated by the pine beetle. You'll also see countertops made from recycled glass, much of it from the park, and recycled fly ash, which is a by-product of coal burning. In addition, there's LED lighting and low-flow toilets. Canyon Lodge is open from the beginning of June through early October.

To make reservations for lodging inside Yellowstone National Park, go online to yellowstonenationalparklodges.com or call (866) 439-7375.

ROB WOOD

ROB WOOD

48 HOURS IN YELLOWSTONE

Only have 48 hours? Make the most of your time by visiting some of our favorite spots in the park.

SEE MAMMOTH HOT SPRINGS

Walk along a mile-long boardwalk to see the colorful travertine terraces formed by hot springs rising to the surface and depositing dissolved limestone in dramatic, staircase-like patterns. From these Lower Terraces, you can reach the Upper Terraces via a staircase.

STROLL MIDWAY AND LOWER GEYSER BASINS

Head to Midway Geyser Basin and walk along the boardwalk to see one of the world's largest, deepest hot springs, Grand Prismatic Spring. It's larger than a football field at 370 feet across and deeper than a ten-story building at 125 feet.

WATCH OLD FAITHFUL

Take a seat and watch the world's most famous geyser. It erupts about twenty times a day. The front desk of the Old Faithful Inn posts eruption times.

DINE AT OLD FAITHFUL INN

A trip to Yellowstone would not be complete without seeing the largest log structure in the world, the Old Faithful Inn built from 1903 to 1904. Breakfast and lunch are first-come, first-served, but you need to make dinner reservations in advance. Can't get dinner reservations? Have a drink and appetizers in the Bear Pit Lounge.

WAKE UP WITH THE WOLVES

For your best chance of seeing a wolf, get up before sunrise and head to the Lamar Valley in the park's northeast corner. Use your binoculars or scope at the roadside pullouts and you may see bears, bison, deer, and osprey.

EAT AT ROOSEVELT LODGE

Built in 1920, Roosevelt Lodge, one of the park's most charming and intimate restaurants, has a wonderful front porch with rocking chairs where you can have a drink and take in park views. Inside, the log building is wonderfully authentic with food for every dietary need.

CRUISE TOWER ROAD AND HIKE MT. WASHBURN

Head south from Roosevelt and stop at the 132-foot Tower Fall. Continue to drive up the 8,859-foot Dunraven Pass. At the top, park and hike the 3.1-mile (one way) trail to Mt. Washburn's 10,243-foot summit.

VIEW WILDLIFE IN THE HAYDEN VALLEY

This grassy valley supports huge herds of bison, grizzly bears, elk, coyotes, wolves, moose, and bald eagles. Stop at one of the pullouts, especially at dawn or dusk, to see these iconic Yellowstone animals with binoculars or a scope.

NICK COTE

PACKING LIST

You are headed to Yellowstone National Park, where you will find half of the world's geysers and more wildlife than anywhere else in the Lower 48. From high mountain peaks to green valleys and alpine rivers, there are hundreds of places to explore. But how do you pack for Yellowstone? Here are the most essential items.

BINOCULARS OR A SPOTTING SCOPE

Don't miss seeing that grizzly across Hayden Valley or the wolf trotting through the grass in the Lamar Valley. Bring along a good pair of binoculars or a spotting scope to see all the wildlife Yellowstone has to offer. It's worth talking to your local camping store employee about the different types of binoculars for sale as not all are created equal. You don't want to end up with an extraordinarily weak pair, nor a pair too heavy to hike with. **Photo tip:** Put your cell phone camera up to the spotting scope lens to take a close-up shot of the herd of moose in the distance.

BEAR SPRAY

The Greater Yellowstone region is home to about 700 grizzlies, so bear spray is a must in Yellowstone if you plan on doing any sort of hiking or walking on trails. The park advises everyone on the trails to carry bear spray and know how to use it in the event you encounter a grizzly. You can purchase bear spray at camping stores (don't try to bring it on the plane) in the towns near the park, or you can rent it from the kiosk at the Canyon Village Visitor Center. Keep in mind, the best prevention is going to visitor centers to find out what areas to avoid, walking in groups of three or more, keeping at least 100 yards between you and a bear, and making noise as you hike to avoid surprising a bear. (See the sidebar on page 27 for more information.)

A SUN HAT, SUNGLASSES, AND SUNSCREEN

You only need to have experienced the sun in the West one time before you realize how strong it really is, especially since Yellowstone sits at an average elevation of 8,000 feet. Bring a wide-brimmed hat, which is preferable over a baseball cap, to cover your entire face. Then, apply sunscreen over all exposed skin, including the back of your neck. Sunglasses will protect your eyes from being burned, and polarized lenses will help you see views more clearly. Don't forget, you are 8,000 feet closer to the sun than at sea level. Purchase sunglasses straps if you plan to be on the water.

There are lots of places to hike in and around Yellowstone National Park. Just make sure you pack all the right items.
GRANT ORDELHEIDE

STURDY HIKING BOOTS

To make the most out of your trip, pack a pair of supportive, waterproof, and breathable hiking boots. The advantage to boots over athletic shoes is the hard, unyielding sole that will protect your feet as you walk over rocky surfaces. Boots will allow you to navigate wet and dry trails with ease and enable you to explore farther than you otherwise would have.

A RAIN JACKET

Who brings a rain jacket to the dry West? Everyone should because in the summer, afternoon rainstorms roll in almost like clockwork. The good news is they pass quickly. The bad news is the temperature drops dramatically when it rains, turning a warm day into one that feels freezing. When it rains and temperatures plummet, you want a jacket that can keep you warm and dry.

A COUPLE WATER BOTTLES OR A HYDRATION SYSTEM

The average elevation of Yellowstone National Park is 8,000 feet. Combat the effects of high elevation and sun by drinking water almost constantly. Because the air is dry, your sweat quickly evaporates. Often, you won't know you are sweating. Drinking water ensures you won't get dehydrated, which can lead to headaches and more serious conditions like heat cramps and heat stroke. Plan to drink .5–1 liter per hour of hiking. Even when you are not recreating, be sure to keep drinking. If your urine is clear, you are hydrated. Hydration packs allow you to keep sipping even as you are on the move.

WARM AND COLD CLOTHING LAYERS

When you are sitting in sweltering heat in Chicago, it may seem totally ridiculous to pack a winter hat and warm layers for your Yellowstone trip. Ignore your inner cynic. At 8,000 feet, park temperatures can fluctuate 30 degrees in 1 day, going from 40 degrees F in the night to 70 degrees F in the day. Be sure to pack light layers for daytime and others that will keep you warm in the evenings, including a winter hat and a down jacket, for when the sun sets and cooler air moves in. You will be surprised at how quickly temperatures drop as the sun sets.

A STAR CHART

You'll find some very dark skies in Yellowstone, which is hundreds of miles from major cities. With a star chart, you'll be able to identify some of the formations you may never have seen before, especially if you are coming from an urban environment. Or use technology and download the SkyView free app for iPhone or Android. You may be able to see up to 15,000 stars in the Wyoming sky in comparison to 500 in an urban sky. It's far out!

STURDY WATER SHOES

If you plan on river rafting, canoeing, or kayaking, you will want a good pair of water shoes. Flip-flops are not recommended for water activities as they will get stuck in the mud and either break or get swallowed down river. A covered rubber-toed shoe can help you avoid getting bruised toes from river rocks or cuts from stray logs.

GRANT ORDELHEIDE

A TABLECLOTH

It's the little things that make a big difference. When you stop at the road-side weathered picnic table to eat lunch, pull out your tablecloth to go from down-home to gourmet in a matter of seconds. You'll also avoid getting hard-to-remove splinters when you lean against the table.

BUG SPRAY

Spend more time enjoying the scenery rather than swatting bugs. If you don't want to use traditional formulas that include strong chemicals, there are plenty of bug sprays available these days that are made from natural ingredients and are safer for use by children.

DAYPACK

Make going for a stroll at Mammoth Hot Springs or a longer hike to Fairy Falls easier with a daypack. Place all your (and your family's) essentials like extra layers, extra snacks, a flashlight, binoculars, and simple first-aid kit in it.

HEADLAMP

Read at night in your tent comfortably with your headlamp or use it to safely walk to and from evening ranger talks.

DOWNLOAD SIGHTSEEING APPS

You're less likely to miss the highlights of the areas you are driving by if you listen to the GyPSy Guide. The tour app uses your device's location abilities to play the commentary automatically as you drive, recommending places worth pulling over for and providing background stories.

To find out when various geysers are estimated to erupt, download the free National Park Service Yellowstone Geysers app from iTunes or Google Play. You do need Wi-Fi or cell phone service, which can be spotty in the park, to access the predictions.

PLASTIC BAGS

Plastic bags come in handy to pack out used toilet paper if nature calls while you are hiking. It's a big no-no to try to bury toilet paper in the backcountry. It has to be packed out.

WILDLIFE OF YELLOWSTONE

There's a lot of wildlife to see in and around Yellowstone if you know where to look for it. When viewing bears and wolves, keep a safe distance of at least 100 yards between you and the animals. With all other wildlife, keep a distance of at least 25 yards.

↓ BISON

Roughly 4,600 bison roam in Yellowstone. At the turn of the 20th century, America's wild bison, which at one time numbered 60 million, had dwindled to about two dozen animals. The bison in Yellowstone today are descendants of those survivors. Bison can weigh up to 2,000 pounds, and although they may seem docile, they are unpredictable animals and have been known to charge at visitors who approach them too closely.

WHERE TO SEE THEM: In Yellowstone, check out the Lamar and Hayden Valleys. Both are great places to watch bison. Also, look for them near Pelican Valley. In Grand Teton, look for them along the Snake River from Jackson Lake Dam south to Moose.

ROB WOOD

↑ BLACK BEAR

These omnivores can weigh up to 400 pounds and stretch from 2 to 4 feet tall. They can be black, blond, or brown, which can lead visitors to misidentify them as grizzlies. They follow their mostly vegetarian food sources up and down the park. In spring, they feast on shrubs and new shoots in the forest. Throughout summer and fall, they retreat to the cooler alpine zone, chasing berries and trout. Black bears hibernate during winter and mate during the summer. Litters typically consist of two cubs.

WHERE TO SEE THEM: In Yellowstone, see them in the Lamar and Hayden Valleys. In Grand Teton, look for them in Two Ocean and Emma Mathilde Lakes, Colter Bay, and Teton Park Road.

→ ELK

In summer, Yellowstone houses about 10,000–20,000 elk. The population drops to 5,000 in winter. Many area elk winter in the National Elk Refuge near Jackson. Adult bull elk weigh up to 700 pounds, while adult females may weigh up to 500 pounds. Their rear ends are white and often give them away to passersby. Elk congregate at lower elevations during mating season, also known as "the rut," from September to October, making fall the best time to spot them.

WHERE TO SEE THEM: See elk throughout Yellowstone, especially near Mammoth Hot Springs, Lamar Valley, Norris Junction, Gibbon River, and Madison Junction. In Grand Teton, they gather near Teton Park Road, in Willow Flats, Two Ocean and Emma Mathilde Lakes, and along the Snake River from Jackson Lake Dam south to Moose.

GRANT ORDELHEIDE

↑ GRIZZLY BEAR

Grizzlies, also referred to as "brown bears," have a distinctive hump between their shoulders, a long snout, and short, fuzzy ears that are smaller than those of black bears. Their front claws measure between 2 and 4 inches in length. They can reach 4 feet at the shoulder and can weigh up to 700 pounds. They typically have blonde-tipped fur on their backs and flanks. The Yellowstone region is home to about 700 grizzlies.

WHERE TO SEE THEM: Yellowstone's grizzlies often wander through the Lamar and Hayden Valleys, around Yellowstone Lake, Heart Lake, and Pelican Valley. In Grand Teton National Park, look for them in Willow Flats, Two Ocean and Emma Mathilde Lakes, Oxbow Bend, and Cascade and Death Canyons.

HOW TO AVOID RUNNING INTO A BEAR

Grizzly bear encounters are rare, but you should always respect these wild and potentially dangerous animals. There's an average of one bear attack per year in Yellowstone, although in both 2011 and 2015, the annual death total was three. Protect yourself on your visit. Visitors should stay at least 100 yards away from bears.

ISTOCK

Before You Explore

Check in with a park visitor center to find out if there has been bear activity on the trails you want to hike and to find out if any areas are closed for bear management. Ask park rangers there for tips on how to avoid a bear encounter.

Purchase or rent bear spray. You can buy it at camping stores or rent it during the summer season at the Yellowstone Canyon Village Visitor Center kiosk. Learn how to use it before you hit the trail.

On the Trail

Stay on the trail, hike in groups of three or more, and talk or sing loudly to reduce your risk of surprising a bear. Ninety-one percent of people who were attacked by bears in Yellowstone since 1970 were hiking alone or with one partner, according to Yellowstone officials. Be alert and look for bear activity to avoid surprising a bear.

Avoid hiking at dawn and dusk and never approach a carcass, as bears may be nearby and ready to defend their food. Never leave a backpack or food unattended as it could attract bears. Always carry bear spray. Keep it accessible on your belt or quick-draw holster.

In Backcountry Camps

Store all food and smelly items like deodorant, sunscreen, and toothpaste in an approved bear canister, bear locker, or hung from a food pole whenever you are not using them. Sleep at least 100 yards from where you prepare and store your food. Never bring or store food in your tent. Avoid cooking very smelly meals (fish or meat).

If You See a Grizzly Bear

Back away slowly and immediately. Never run. In the rare event that the bear charges, stand your ground. Many charges are bluffs with the bear veering away at the last minute. Deploy your bear spray in a wide cloud, aiming slightly downward when the bear is about 60 feet away.

Don't play dead unless the bear knocks you down. In that case, roll on your stomach, put your hands over your neck and lie still.

↑ MOOSE

As the largest member of the deer family, their long snout, bulbous nose, and dewlap under the throat sets them apart from Yellowstone and Grand Teton's other hooved animals. Moose are heavily concentrated in Grand Teton National Park. Look for them in areas full of willows and aquatic vegetation.

WHERE TO SEE THEM: In Yellowstone, look for the park's one hundred or so moose in Willow Park between Norris Junction and Mammoth, and also near Yellowstone Lake, Fishing Bridge, West Thumb, and Hayden Valley. In Grand Teton, see them along Oxbow Bend, Blacktail Ponds, Mormon Row, and Antelope Flats Road.

↓ WOLVES

As of 2016, about ninety-nine wolves roamed in ten packs inside Yellowstone and around its borders, with fifty-eight in the Grand Teton area and about 450 total wolves in the Greater Yellowstone area. These highly social predators, which mainly hunt elk, deer, and bison, have come a long way since 1995, when a reintroduction program brought fourteen Canadian wolves to the park after decades of hunting had effectively wiped the predator out.

WHERE TO SEE THEM: In Yellowstone, the most frequently spotted wolf-packs haunt Lamar Valley, Hayden Valley, the Canyon area, and Blacktail Deer Plateau. Dawn and dusk are the best times to look. In Grand Teton, see them in Willow Flats.

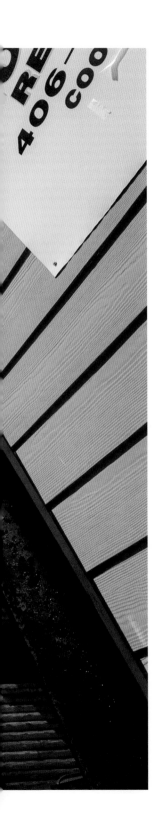

Yellowstone National Park has five entrances. The original entrance is in the north at Gardiner. Fifty-six miles east of Gardiner is another entrance at Cooke City. These two entrances are the least busy of the five, at least as far as people are concerned. (As a matter of fact, some of the best wildlife watching in the park is near these northern entrances.)

Gardiner and the other communities in Paradise Valley and Cooke City are just fine with their relative lack of bustle. If these two entrances were busier, Gardiner would not be the quirky town of 875 inhabitants that it is. Cooke City might have to add on to its historic one-room schoolhouse. Livingston's blue-collar roots would probably succumb to the cowboy cosmopolitanism of Jackson a hundred miles to the south. Real estate prices in Red Lodge, where there's a ski area with no lines and a 900,000-acre wilderness just a short drive from town, would be triple what they are. If you're looking to experience authentic Montana in addition to Yellowstone, the north and northeast entrances are where you want to head.

ROAD TRIP 1
GARDINER

Gardiner has a population of about 875 people. The elk herd that lives nearby numbers more than 3,000. This town sits right at Yellowstone's North Entrance, enabling quick access to the park. It's 100 percent full of character . . . and characters. It's also the only gateway community from which you can drive a car (versus snowmobile) in the park year-round.

The town of Gardiner is named after the highly successful fur trapper Johnson Gardner, who was active in the area from the 1820s until the mid-1830s. Around 1835, members of the Arikara agricultural Indian tribe who lived in the plains north and east of what became Yellowstone National Park killed Gardner after he and some companions had killed three of their tribesmen for killing their friend Hugh Glass (the protagonist in the 2015 film *The Revenant*). In 1870, Gardner the town became Gar*din*er when the Langford-Washburn-Doan Expedition came through the area. They made detailed maps but didn't bother double-checking their spellings. The spelling of the Gardner River in Yellowstone was not corrupted, so the Gardner River is just south of the town of Gardiner and both are named after the same man.

Roosevelt Arch

The Roosevelt Arch was built in 1903 because the powers that be worried Yellowstone's main entrance lacked the pomp and circumstance required to welcome visitors to the world's first national park. It was named after President Teddy Roosevelt, who traveled to Yellowstone for a 2-week vacation and placed the arch's cornerstone. About this vacation, Roosevelt said, "For the last 18 months I have taken everything as it came, from coal strikes to trolley cars, and I feel I am entitled to a fortnight to myself." (Since he was in the park in late April, when it was still buried beneath several feet of snow, it's likely he really did have a fortnight to himself!) Roosevelt was in Gardiner and placed the cornerstone 2 months into construction, in

LOCAL LOWDOWN
SANDY BIERLE, owner of Flying Pig Adventure Company

Sandy and Steve Bierle, both wildlife biologists, went to college in Missoula and "fell in love with Montana," Sandy says. But after graduation, they couldn't find year-round jobs in the state. "With wildlife degrees, the work is often seasonal," Sandy says. The couple ended up in South Dakota and "throughout our time there we were gunning to get back to Montana," says Sandy, who's originally from the Midwest. Thanks to family connections, they learned the Faerbers, who had founded Flying Pig Adventure Company in Gardiner, were looking to sell their business, so the Bierles bought it in 2011. Steve died in 2015 and Sandy now runs the business herself, with the help of the Gardiner community, "the best staff in the world," and her three tween/teenage sons. *511 Scott St. West, (406) 848-7510, flyingpigrafting.com*

Q: *Was buying the business and moving to Gardiner a difficult choice?*

SANDY BIERLE: Since we had three boys, we wanted to make sure it was a good fit. Gardiner is a bit unusual. When we came out for a visit though, one night we were sitting in the Boiling River, the full moon was coming up, and it just all came together. We knew we wanted this epic for our kids.

Q: *Did you think about selling the business and leaving after Steve's death?*

SB: Never. I was like 100 percent "no." The town of Gardiner–it's quirky and full of characters and it's not always pleasant, but it's full of the best people. I didn't want to be anywhere else. It was after Steve died that I

decided to put down roots and get a home here. I built a house on the river with my architect brother.

Q: *Were you a big rafting person before you bought the business?*

SB: Being a marine biologist, I was always in love with the water. I wasn't a skilled technician in terms of whitewater rafting, but we loved it. Steve added the guided fishing.

Q: *What about your boys?*

SB: They're sort of river rats. They spend all their days on the water.

Q: *Do they work at Flying Pig?*

SB: The shop becomes our home base in the summer. We're there all the time with our extended family–the guides and staff. I work with all of these kids in their 20s and they've just been a lifeline to me. When Steve died, so many came back because they wanted to contribute. I hire people with different backgrounds and this gives my kids exposure to people from all over the world who share a common passion.

Q: *Is rafting the Yellowstone River scary?*

SB: The main trip we do is not really extreme in terms of rapids; it works very well for families and people who want to get a little wet but don't want the adrenaline rush of big water. We do a longer trip once a day–or as an overnight–that goes through Yankee Jim Canyon and that section has some higher waves–some upper Class III and once in a while low IV rapids. It's a little more exciting and more intense.

GRANT ORDELHEIDE

April 1903. He never again visited Gardiner and so never saw the completed arch. The arch took 7 months to build.

Architect Robert Reamer, who also designed Old Faithful Inn and Canyon Hotel in the park, designed the arch. The original design for the arch was even grander than what was built and included two ponds and a waterfall, which were never constructed. As Roosevelt laid the cornerstone, a time capsule was placed inside the arch. Some of the items in the time capsule include a 1903 edition of the *World's Almanac*, the 1902 *Proceedings of the Grand Lodge of Montana*, a copy of the Northern Pacific Railway marketing pamphlet for 1903, US coins, copies of the Livingston daily papers, and a Bible.

Red's Blue Goose and Rosie's Deck

High school sweethearts Red and Rosie Curtis survived the Dust Bowl and Great Depression in northeast Oklahoma. And then World War II happened. Red went into the Army. When he got out, "there were no jobs," says his son Chuck. "He started driving trucks across the country." On one trip, Red–he had bright red hair–stopped in Laurel, Montana. In a cafe there, he got to

←YELLOWSTONE RIVER

At 692 miles, it's the longest undammed river in the continental United States. It's the principal tributary of the upper Missouri River. There is no trail going to its headwaters, which are fed by snowfields above 10,000 feet in the Absaroka Range. It flows into (and out of) Yellowstone Lake. It thunders over three ginormous drops, one 109 feet, the next 308 feet, and the last 132 feet. It is considered one of the greatest trout streams in the world. On a sandstone formation overlooking this river near Billings, you can still see the etched "signature" of William Clark, of Lewis and Clark fame. "It" is the Yellowstone River.

Returning east after reaching the Pacific Ocean, William Clark became the first white man to explore the Yellowstone. Native Americans had been using it for millennia. The name is believed to come from the Minnetaree Indian name *Mi tse a-da-zi*, which means "Yellow Rock River." Lewis and Clark translated it as Yellow Stone, and that's what stuck.

---

chatting with a local gentleman, who couldn't stop talking about working for the railroad. "My dad walked into the Northern Pacific office right then and started working for the railroad right away," Chuck says. Rosie moved out to Livingston and Red worked for the railroad, on the passenger service from Livingston to Gardiner, until about 1963. The family then returned to Oklahoma to take care of aging parents. "I've spent almost every summer of my life I can remember in Paradise Valley though," Chuck says.

In the early 1990s, Red and Rosie were bored of retirement, and of Oklahoma. They and Chuck began looking for some sort of business in Gardiner, Montana. "We chose Montana because we knew it," Chuck says. They bought the Blue Goose Saloon. "I am told it was the original post office in town," Chuck says. Red was always told that the saloon was founded by Air Force veterans after World War II. "He was told 'Blue Goose' was the name of a bomber those guys flew. Since he was Red, we changed the name to 'Red's Blue Goose.'"

Although the name changed, little else did. And it's stayed that way in the decades since. "When you walk into the Blue Goose it's like walking back in time," Chuck says. Except for the beer selection and food. The former is heavy on local craft brews and the latter might be cow or bison from a local rancher.

Adjacent to the Blue Goose is Rosie's Deck, which is lined with rocking chairs and "is the nicest view in Gardiner," Chuck says. "Animals literally walk by right underneath it." At Rosie's, you can order drinks, but no food is served there. You're allowed to bring your own though. "To be up there at night, looking at the moon and hearing coyotes howl, it will send chills down your spine." *206 W. Park St., (406) 848-7434*

LOCAL LOWDOWN
DANNY BIERSCHWALE, Director of Strategic Partnerships at Yellowstone Forever Institute

Danny Bierschwale lived in seven or eight different states when he was growing up. His dad was a minister. "When I was in diapers, my dad was working for an organization called A Christian Ministry in the National Parks," Danny says. "He was based in Cooke City. I think that gave me a deep-rooted connection to the park." Danny's dad was moved from Cooke City before Danny was old enough to appreciate the area, but "we visited the park when I was older and I remember seeing bears and bison and the thermal features," he says. During college, Danny worked as a resident coordinator managing a dorm in the Old Faithful area. "That experience that summer really helped further my connection to the natural world and national parks." Danny moved to Gardiner full time in 2007 to work for the Yellowstone Association, which merged with the Yellowstone Park Foundation in 2016 to become Yellowstone Forever Institute. Yellowstone Forever Institute is the official nonprofit partner of Yellowstone National Park. At Yellowstone Forever Institute, Danny is director of strategic partnerships, and in awe that he's found a job with an office directly across from the Roosevelt Arch.

Q: *Can you see any wild animals out your window right now?*

DANNY BIERSCHWALE: There are some bison roaming around. That is a very unique aspect of where we live. I often feel like I'm living in the show *Northern Exposure*. We don't actually get moose so often, but we get every other variety of wildlife. Right now there's a fox that has been hanging around. It's great to see it, but hopefully he'll move on eventually. You never want wildlife to get used to humans. That's when problems start.

Q: *Have you ever been trapped in your house by bison or elk in your front yard or something?*

DB: I've often walked out my front door and had elk grazing on the trees in the yard. When I first moved here, I remember looking out my back window and watching a bear and a couple of cubs that had climbed onto the roof of the gas station behind my house. I sat there and watched them for a while.

Q: *If you don't go hiking in Yellowstone, where do you go?*

DB: I will often recreate in the national forest surrounding the national park. I can bring my dog with me there; you can't bring dogs hiking in the park. There is an old mining town just outside of Gardiner called Jardine and it provides quick and easy access to the Beartooth Wilderness. I'll often go up near Eagle Creek and Bear Creek.

GRANT ORDELHEIDE

Whether you have a day or 3 weeks or are interested in geology, history, wildflowers, or wild animals, Yellowstone Forever Institute has a class for you. Based in Gardiner in the former Yellowstone Association building, the institute offers hundreds of programs annually and has something for almost all ages. In one of the institute's overnight field seminars, learn alongside experts like wildlife biologists, artists, geothermal scientists, or photographers and then hang out at the historic Lamar Buffalo Ranch Field Campus in the park's remote northeastern corner. *308 E. Park St., (406) 848-2400, www.yellowstone.org*

ROAD TRIP 2
ENCOUNTERING LOCAL CHARACTERS

There's archaeological evidence showing Paradise Valley has been continuously occupied for 12,600 years. It is possible its current crop of residents is its most interesting though. On any given day, you could run into Earl Craig, Montana's poet laureate who works as a farrier—that's someone who shoes horses—when not writing poetry; Margot Kidder, known in the wider world as Lois Lane in four *Superman* movies in the 1970s and 1980s, and locally for being one of dozens of protesters arrested on the steps of the White House in a protest of the Keystone XL pipeline; or John Bailey, the fly-fishing expert who coached Brad Pitt in casting for the movie *A River Runs Through It*. And then there are all of the writers and movie stars (Jeff Bridges met his wife Susan while he was filming a movie at Chico Hot Springs, where she worked as a waitress at the time). Since the latter are often in Livingston to lay low, we're not going to mention them. But, if you're in a bar and think the person next to you looks like Michael Keaton, it very well might be.

LYNN DONALDSON PHOTOGRAPHY

↑ Yellowstone Gateway Museum

While Livingston is plenty interesting these days, it's worth taking time to get to know its past, especially when its past is on exhibit in a school built in 1907 and is now listed on the National Register of Historic Places. A visit to the Yellowstone Gateway Museum is worth it just to get a peek inside the North Side School, which the museum has kept mostly intact. "We're an old school with four big classrooms, so we have four main exhibits," says museum director Paul Shea. When Paul came on as the Gateway Museum's director in 2009, he had the task of re-exhibiting the museum's entire collection. Within the four main permanent exhibits, on Native American cultures, expeditions, transportation, and pioneer life, he "uses objects to enhance the story line, rather than the object being the story. And every exhibit has to have a children's component. It's not just a museum for adults," says Paul, who first came to the area in 1979 to work a summer in Yellowstone. "I came up and hit Yellowstone and it was like getting hit upside the head. Yellowstone chooses her own and when she chooses you, you don't get away. It changed my life, and, as this museum shows, the lives of countless others. To me, and a lot of people, Yellowstone is a spiritual place." *118 West Chinook St., (406) 222-4184, yellowstonegatewaymuseum.org*

LOCAL LOWDOWN
TIM CAHILL, Writer

Tim Cahill's journey to becoming a travel writer was circuitous. First, he traded law school for a master's degree in creative writing. Then, while studying for the latter at San Francisco State, he climbed up Mt. Tam and played dead. This was in service of researching turkey vultures, which eventually began to circle overhead. A photographer friend needed Tim to write an article to accompany some bird images he wanted to send to the *San Francisco Examiner*. Naturally, with such unorthodox research methods, the resulting article was a hit with the newspaper's editor and Tim was asked for more.

Within a year, Tim was hired on at what was then a nascent *Rolling Stone* magazine. For 7 years, he worked alongside the likes of Hunter S. Thompson, Tim Farris, and David Felton, helping to usher in a movement called New Journalism. When *Rolling Stone* moved to New York, Tim stayed in San Francisco and became a founding editor of *Outside* magazine. Tim quickly became one of the magazine's star writers, having convinced the publisher that readers would love an international adventure column and that he was the perfect man for the job. When *Outside* moved to Chicago, Tim went freelance, which, at the time, was every bit as unorthodox as his ornithological research methods.

Since then, Tim has written hundreds of articles for *National Geographic*, *Life*, *Travel & Leisure*, *Reader's Digest*, *Esquire*, the *New York Times Book Review*, and even *Yoga Journal*. He's contracted malaria, fallen off cliffs, investigated the murder of an American in the jungles of Peru, and set a Guinness World Record for the fastest Pan-American traverse, all while introducing readers to new people and places. He has won a Lowell Thomas Gold Award, a National Magazine Award, and his work has been included in *Best American Travel Writing* three times. Tim has written nine books. His first, *Buried Dreams*, a true-crime account of the serial killer John Wayne Gacy, was a national bestseller. The *San Francisco Chronicle* wrote that if anything could inspire the most slothful of couch potatoes to get out there for an adventure, it would be his book *Hold the Enlightenment*.

Tim's first screenplay was for the IMAX film *Everest*, which became one of the top 20 films of 1998 and bested *Titanic* in per-screen ticket sales. Another screenplay he co-authored, for the documentary film *The Living Sea*, was nominated for an Academy Award. Tim has lived in Livingston since 1979.

Q: *How is Livingston the same as it was in 1979?*

TIM CAHILL: The population is about the same—about 7,000 in the town and 16,000 in the county—and you find all kinds of different and interesting people in town. You might walk into someone who just got back from a fact-finding mission to North Korea or someone who speaks Arabic and knows the Koran.

Q: *Any drawbacks of living here?*

TC: The wind. It can blow for 3 days. By some accounts, this is the windiest town in America. We have regular gusts to 70 or 80 miles per hour. We've had the wind literally blow an empty freight car off the railroad track. The wind can get to you; it's a psychological thing. It depletes you of serotonin.

Q: *Did you ever think about leaving?*

TC: Not really. Here's a little something from sports. People talk about lifting weights and they say you are not really going to be able to do a snatch and jerk in a canoe. You need a solid base. Once you have the solid base, then you can lift the weights over your head. That's the way I like to think of our little community. It is very solid.

Q: *How is Livingston different than it was in 1979?*

TC: The two bars that I used to go to were the Wrangler and the Long Branch. They had live music pretty much every night and it wasn't unusual to have an actual fistfight in the alley behind the bar. One of those bars is now the Katabatic Brewery, which makes craft beer, and one is Jalisco's Mexican restaurant. And if there is a fistfight on the street today, both participants will be taken to jail and will have to deal with assault charges.

Q: *Did you ever get in any fistfights?*

TC: I'm good at running away from fights.

Chico Hot Springs

Chico Hot Springs in the tiny town of Pray, at the end of a county road and at the base of Emigrant Peak, has only had five owners since Bill and Percie Knowles founded it as a boardinghouse for miners in 1900. Seabring Davis and her husband, Colin, are the current owners. Colin started as the general manager at Chico in 1995 and he and Seabring bought it in 2016. Prior to their purchase, Mike and Eve Art owned it for 45 years. They get the credit for making Chico the Montana institution it is today. In 1972, algae grew in the hot spring pools, and other parts of the resort were worse off. Mike and Eve and their daughters, Jackie and Andrea, moved out west from Cleveland, Ohio—Mike discovered the property while in Montana on a hunting trip—and began fixing the place up. They started with the dining room. Mike believed that if they served the best food in the state, that would draw visitors. He was right, but the cleaned-up pool and refreshed rooms didn't hurt either. There are menu items that date to the earliest days of the Arts' ownership that Seabring calls "Chico classics": the beef Wellington entree for two, the flaming orange dessert, and the pine nut–crusted halibut. Almost any night, whatever the season, Chico's dining room is full. So are its rooms. *163 Chico Rd., (406) 333-4933, www.chicohotsprings.com*

The Northern Pacific caboose available for nightly rental at Chico was meant to be a writing studio for Seabring. "My husband bought it at auction," she says. "He thought it was a super score to bring me this dream of my writing studio. But I don't want a caboose in my backyard in my house in town." So Colin came up with another idea: move it to Chico and make it a custom guest room. It was an empty shell when he bought it, so they were able to completely design it. The floors are cherry. There's a giant soaking tub, the wallpaper is a red Victorian pattern, and the stained glass windows and light fixtures are from the Victorian era. "It doesn't feel like you're in a caboose, but a luxury train car from the early 1900s," Seabring says. *163 Chico Rd., [406] 333-4933, www.chicohotsprings.com/accommodations/caboose*

Q: *Do you remember the first time you came to Chico?*

SEABRING DAVIS: Yes, I was in college in Bozeman, so it was around 1990. I remember exactly what we ate and I remember the wine, and, since I later worked as a waitress in the restaurant, I remember the table number we sat at. I didn't marry the guy I came with, so it wasn't special in the sense that I still have a relationship with the person, but I still have a relationship with the place.

Q: *So what'd you eat?*

SD: We had the beef Wellington, which is only available in service for two and is carved tableside. I had never eaten anything like that before. Then we had the flaming orange for dessert. It's a frozen orange filled with ice cream and other goodies and lined with chocolate and set on fire tableside. Staff calls that combo "the classic." It will always be the same. For so many people, this is what their image of eating at Chico's is like and that's why we won't change it.

Q: *How often do you soak in the mineral pool now that you own it?*

SD: I probably go once a week. I love to go in the winter. Locals' favorite time to go is winter just because it is so great to have the steam coming off the water into the cold air.

Q: *There are lots of different room types for overnight guests. Do you have a favorite?*

SD: Room 101 is in the old hotel. It is kind of funny because it's right adjacent to the lobby. Most people would think it would be too noisy. But what is cool about it is that it has velvet flock bordello wallpaper and one of the old brass beds that is original to the property, which is 1900. This little room epitomizes what Chico is historically.

Q: *Do you feel pressure as the owners of such a beloved piece of history?*

SD: Chico is everybody's place and we do feel the responsibility of maintaining it to match the memories of so many people that have visited. I don't know how many old-timers I've met that have told me their first job was at Chico back when they were 15 in the 1960s or however long ago. I've heard from people that Chico is the reason they moved to Montana, that it made them look at the state differently. We're very aware, and we feel this ourselves, that it's not just a place you come to have a great meal and stay on the way to somewhere else.

CHICO'S PINE NUT–CRUSTED HALIBUT
SERVES 4 PEOPLE

PINE NUT CRUST

2 cups pine nuts

1 cup breadcrumbs

1 teaspoon salt

⅓ cup parsley

PORT WINE BUTTER

2 cups port wine

1 cup heavy whipping cream

8 tablespoons (1 stick) butter

MANGO SALSA
(YIELDS 2 CUPS)

1 mango, peeled, seeded, and diced

1 small red onion, diced

1 red bell pepper, diced

1 bunch chopped chives

3 tablespoons raspberry vinegar

2 tablespoons honey

2 tablespoons chopped cilantro

HALIBUT

1 teaspoon olive oil

1 cup buttermilk

1 cup flour

4 6-ounce halibut fillets

CHICO'S

PREPARATION

PINE NUT CRUST

In a food processor, add all ingredients. Pulse until nuts are diced, but not too fine; remove and set aside. You may also prepare the crust by hand. Be sure to dice the nuts before combining with other ingredients.

PORT WINE BUTTER

This sauce cannot be reheated or chilled, so prepare it just before the main course is in the oven. Reduce port over medium heat until it forms a syrup (about 20 minutes). When it coats a metal spoon, it is ready. Add cream, reduce until thick. Remove from heat and add butter, stirring constantly until melted and smooth. Turn heat down to low and use promptly.

MANGO SALSA

Mix all ingredients together in a bowl and refrigerate until needed.

HALIBUT

Preheat the oven to 400 degrees. Place buttermilk, flour, and pine nut mixture in separate bowls and arrange in a row on the counter. Dip fillets on one side only in flour, buttermilk, and then add pine nuts. On the stove, heat a pan with a touch of olive oil (teaspoon) and with crust-side down sauté the fish until nuts are golden brown. Place the sautéed fish on a greased baking dish, crust-side up, and bake in the oven for 8 to 10 minutes.

Present the halibut in a pool of port wine butter sauce, topped with the fresh mango salsa.

ROAD TRIP 3
A TRIP TO PARADISE

Paradise Valley comes by its name honestly. On the flat land between the craggy Absaroka Mountains and the Gallatin Range, the Yellowstone River winds through an agrarian landscape. It was this valley that was the original entrance to Yellowstone.

While the number of ranches in the valley has declined, the valley's wild lands have not. Much of the valley is part of the 1.8-million-acre Gallatin National Forest, which has more than 3,000 miles of hiking trails and forty

drive-to campgrounds and is home to 300-some species of animals, including grizzly bears and wolves. Livingston is home to the forest's Yellowstone Ranger District, which covers Paradise Valley and even goes north to the Crazy Mountains.

Emigrant Peak

Livingston outdoor store Timber Trails maintains a series of handouts on its staff's favorite hikes. Emigrant Peak is one of them. You can stop into the shop to get a copy of the handout this description is adapted from. *309 W. Park St., (406) 222-9550, timbertrailsmontana.com*

Emigrant is the distinctive peak that stands out from the main body of the Absaroka Range. Its 10,921-foot summit provides exceptional views of the crest of the Absarokas, Lone Peak, and, away to the south, the Tetons.

Start at the Gold Prize Creek trailhead. Drive 1.5 miles up Six Mile Creek Road to a signed left turn; the trailhead is a short distance farther. Walk past the road closure. The old road quickly becomes a trail. After walking on the old road through part of the 1,200 acres that burned in July 1999 in the Six Mile drainage, the trail begins to steepen. Don't expect it to mellow out anytime soon. Stay left and climb steeply through sage and scattered stands of pine and fir toward a large meadow. From here, there are gorgeous views down onto Paradise Valley. Continue hiking along a fence line at the meadow boundary. Beyond the fence, you'll climb through a grove of fir and whitebark pine. At this point, you'll be nearing tree line. Continue to follow the obvious ridgeline. Here, sometimes there is a trail and sometimes there is not. The ridge is a combination of boulders, scree, and alpine tundra to the summit.

Not that anyone is counting, but, on a clear day, from the top of Emigrant, you can see twelve different mountain ranges: the Absarokas, the Beartooths, the Crazies, the Castle Mountains, the Big Belts, the Bridger Range, the Gallatins and Madisons, the Gravely Range, the Tobacco Roots, the Pioneer Mountains, and the Tetons. And, of course, you can see Yellowstone National Park too.

Emigrant Peak is named for the hundreds of miners who emigrated to the area beneath this peak in the mid-1860s looking for gold. It was in 1863 that prospector Thomas Curry discovered gold in a creek on the east side of the peak. The gulch this creek flows in was first called "Curry's Gulch" but today is known as Emigrant Gulch.

LOCAL LOWDOWN

DALE SEXTON, Founder of Timber Trails

Dale Sexton was born and raised in Livingston and in 1996 founded Timber Trails, an outdoor store in a historic building in downtown. The shop "sells stuff to survive, but our foundation is providing information to people first and foremost," Dale says. Since it opened, the shop has doubled in size. Still, Dale says, "we're surviving on our growth, but we're thriving with what this business enables us to do." *309 W. Park St., (406) 222-9550, timbertrailsmontana.com*

Q: So what does the business enable you to do?

DALE SEXTON: Yesterday I went skiing with my older daughter's fifth-grade class, and today I was in the classroom helping out. Annually I take my girls on a bike trip where we just pack up all our stuff and go. I put their old child trailer on my bike and the dog rides in the trailer and we just camp along the route. Last summer, we did our first backpacking trip and we got to the top of Emigrant Peak and Elephanthead Mountain.

COURTESY DALE SEXTON

Q: How did Timber Trails come about?

DS: By the mid-1990s, I was doing more hiking, biking, and skiing than fishing. And Livingston didn't have an outdoor specialty store. I had a building in downtown I had bought in 1992 and was trying to figure out what to do with it.

Q: So fishing was your first love?

DS: Fishing for me goes back to before I could walk. My mom and father were avid worm dunkers and we caught oodles and oodles of fish. It was one of my favorite things growing up. I can recall my father coming home from work, and if I had the fishing gear ready to go, we'd head out for an hour. When I was in fifth grade, I remember him saying, "Boy, it's too bad you can't make a living as a fisherman, because I think you could do good at it." I started guiding in 1983, when I was still in high school. When I was working at Dan Bailey, I got my outfitters license, probably in 1992, or 1993.

Q: Do you still do any fishing or are you all about the other sports now?

DS: I have a few clients that date back to my earliest days of guiding, but they're friends more than clients today. I still have my outfitters license. I probably guide 30 to 40 days a summer. It reenergizes me and gets me out.

Q: What's the most usual information people want when they come into the shop?

DS: They're looking for places to hike or bike. We have an "Our Favorite Hikes" series that we're always adding to. The descriptions of the hikes are a free handout we have here in the shop.

Gallatin Petrified Forest
and Tom Miner Basin

Tom Miner Basin is on Timber Trails' list of favorite hikes. There's wildlife—this is serious grizzly country—but the basin's most unique feature is the Gallatin Petrified Forest. These trees were petrified in an upright position, and, 50 million years later, they're still in that same upright position. The "Petrified Forest Interpretive Trail" starts at the Tom Miner Campground.

If you're more interested in grizzly bears than trees-turned-into-rock, look for them in the large field near the B Bar Ranch headquarters as you're driving down Tom Miner Creek Road. Wild caraway grows here, and grizzlies love to eat its roots. *Tom Miner Creek Road is 35 miles south of Livingston; the trailhead is 10 miles down this road at the Tom Miner Campground; (406) 848-7375, www.fs.usda.gov*

WHICH RIVER RUNS THROUGH IT?

It was one of the many writers who lives in Paradise Valley, Thomas McGuane, who introduced Robert Redford to Norman Maclean's story "A River Runs Through It." Redford then turned it into a feature film of the same name. The story actually takes place in the 1920s in Missoula, with the fishing happening on the Blackfoot River, but that city and river were very different by 1992, when the movie was filmed. Downtown Missoula was no longer all quaint redbrick buildings. The Blackfoot had suffered at the hands of humans. There was the failure of a tailings reservoir that released tons of toxic sediment into its headwaters. Generations of timber harvesting had left mountain creeks and streams full of sediment, and grazing and irrigation had killed much of the native fish population. Redford knew that Livingston had a downtown that, with a little work, could be brought back to the 1920s. And the nearby Gallatin River was a healthy fishery. So Livingston was transformed into 1920s Missoula and the Gallatin River stood in for the Blackfoot. *A River Runs Through It* won the Oscar for best cinematography in 1993. Since the early 1990s, conservation groups have been successfully working to restore the Blackfoot and the river is now close to being the great fishery it once was.

LOCAL LOWDOWN
STEVE HORAN, Photographer of the
People of Yellowstone Project

Photographer Steve Horan knew pretty early into his People of Yellowstone project that he wanted to make a book. He did not know, however, how much work and time goes into making a book. "I thought it'd take 1½ years," he says. "It took 5." *People of Yellowstone*, featuring eighty-five of Steve's photos and text by writer Ruth W. Crocker, was published in spring 2017. Ruth, whose work has been featured in the annual anthology *Best American Essays*, came into the project in year 3. "I thought I'd be able to write it too," Steve says, "but the more

stories I heard, the more I realized I couldn't do the words justice."

Steve first came to Yellowstone in 1985, to visit his brother Jim Horan, who lives in Livingston. "I came out to visit him and fell in love with the place and got a job myself in Yellowstone for the summer. I left after that season, but Jim stayed, so I've now been visiting him for over 30 years–I come out whenever I get the chance." It was Jim who suggested a Yellowstone-based photo project. Steve started his project in 2010, first by photographing people who lived,

JOHN ZUMPANO

worked, and played "strictly in the park," he says. "But it became obvious I couldn't do that. I had to expand. Sure Yellowstone is a national park with distinct boundaries, but its wildlife doesn't recognize those boundaries. It's the whole Greater Yellowstone Ecosystem." So Steve expanded to include people throughout the ecosystem.

He ended up photographing 120 people who work in and around Yellowstone, including wolf biologists, backcountry rangers, volunteers, a Crow tribal elder, wranglers, bellhops, and researchers. "I didn't just go for photos of people standing in a field," Steve says. "I wanted to connect with each subject and to their ideas and what they do." The end result is a book that "helps people understand that this place is magical and that it changes people, for the best, and heals people, and that it's worth something to fight to preserve it for future generations," Steve says. "The more people

outside of this area understand what it takes to make it in a place like this—how people survive here, what characters they are, and how hard it is to make a life here—the better it is. So many people in this area could be somewhere else making a lot of money, but they decide it is the lifestyle and beauty of this area that is what is important."

As diverse as Steve's subjects are, he found commonalities. "Everyone I photographed—and I spent a lot of time talking to them beforehand, getting their stories and learning about their lives—seemed down to earth and connected to nature. There was a general love of life and willingness to explore. It is inspiring and educational to hear all the different ways people connect to this special place." Steve says his subjects ranged in age from 19 to 94 at the time he photographed them. *Peopleof yellowstone.com*

FLY FISHING

According to John Bailey, nowhere has the variety of fishing that Livingston does. There are big rivers like the Yellowstone, which runs right through town and which you can fish year-round. There are spring creeks like Armstrong's, and there are small stream fisheries like Mill Creek. And then there are all the secret spots local fishermen won't dare share for publication.

It makes perfect sense then that Livingston is the headquarters for the International Federation of Fly Fishers. This group works to conserve fly fisheries around the world and educate people about the sport. It also preserves the history of the sport, which it turns out you don't need to be a fly fisherman to appreciate. Included in its collection of thousands of flies, from antique to modern, is one tied by the illustrious British angler Frank Sawyer, who was a river keeper in the early to mid-1900s. (The musician Sting owns one of the sections of river Sawyer was once responsible for.) Sawyer is best remembered as the inventor of sunken nymphs. These flies were unique at the time because they were tied with copper wire, which was heavier than the thread typically used at the time. The museum's collection also includes memorabilia that once belonged to fly-fishing power couple Lee and Joan Wulff and a variety of rods. Lee Wulff is credited with inventing the fishing vest; Joan is considered the best female fly fisherman in the world. *5237 US 89S, Suite 11, (406) 222-9369, www.fedflyfishers.org*

ROAD TRIP 4
RED LODGE

Red Lodge has had ups and downs since its founding in 1884. Today it's on its way up, not that anyone in town would ever say that (its residents are pretty low key). Red Lodge has mining and western histories like many Montana towns and celebrates both. What makes it unique though, especially in the 21st century, is that it is an authentic, unpretentious, undiscovered northern Rockies mountain town. Red Lodge has a ski resort with no lift lines, a main street lined with brick buildings (including one of the West's most classic outdoor gear shops), fly fishing right in downtown, and over 1 million acres of national forest and wilderness right out its back door.

The Pollard Hotel

When the Pollard Hotel was built in 1893 for the then whopping sum of $20,000, it was Red Lodge's first brick building. Opening first as the Spofford Hotel, it didn't become the Pollard until 1902, when Thomas F. Pollard bought the hotel. Pollard almost doubled the size of the hotel, from thirty-five rooms to sixty, and added a bowling alley and barbershop in the basement. The hotel's restaurant was the nicest in town, serving such delicacies as broiled lobster, which was brought to town from the East Coast via train. (The depot was a short distance from the hotel.)

Local celebrities such as Colonel Buffalo Bill Cody, Frederic Remington, William Jennings Bryan, Calamity Jane, and later Ernest Hemingway frequented the hotel. On September 18, 1897, the Sundance Kid robbed Carbon County Bank, which was housed inside the Pollard Hotel. Local lawman John Dunn placed the Sundance Kid under arrest, not once but twice. The second time was after he escaped from the jail in Deadwood, South Dakota.

Mr. Pollard remained in Red Lodge until his death in 1942. His widow ran the hotel for several years, before selling it to Lottie Salk. Over the years, it carried several names: the Chief, the Hotel Tyler, and the Cielo Grande.

In 1991, Hotel Company of Red Lodge bought the hotel and began the Pollard's restoration in accordance with National Park Service guidelines. Efforts paid off when on June 15, 1994, the Pollard Hotel re-opened with a new

Gary Ferguson has written twenty-three books on science and nature, including the award-winning *Hawks Rest: A Season in the Heart of Yellowstone* for which he lived for a summer in one of the most remote spots in the Lower 48 states. Other books include *Decade of the Wolf* (co-written with Douglas Smith), *Shouting at the Sky: Troubled Teens and the Promise of the Wild*, and *Through the Woods: A Journey Through America's Forests*. Ferguson's most recent book is *Land on Fire: The New Reality of Wildfire in the American West*. In January 2017, Ferguson said, "I'm ruminating about my next big project. It will certainly be resting in ecology and the wisdom of science and the wisdom of cultures across thousands of years. They're not as far apart as we sometimes think."

A native of South Bend, Indiana, Ferguson came to Red Lodge, Montana, in 1987 with his wife Jane, who was an environmental educator. "Between her job and me being a nature writer, the idea of moving to the largest intact ecosystem in the temperate world was appealing," Gary says. When Gary and Jane arrived in Red Lodge to check it out, "it was a love affair at first sight. The ecosystem was every bit as magnificent as we imagined. And the people of Red Lodge are interesting and intriguing and supportive of who we are," Gary says. In 2005, when Jane died canoeing in northern Ontario, Red Lodge became even more important to Gary. "The community was a stable, loving base which I could use to find my way out of the darkness of grief." Gary's 2014 book, *The Carry Home*, chronicles the role wilderness played in helping him through his grief and in rediscovering himself. He married cultural psychologist Mary Clare in 2014.

Q: *How did you get started writing?*

GARY FERGUSON: I started writing back around 1981 full time. I was very interested from a young age in the natural world. Could I not write about nature, I do not know if I would have followed the writing path.

Q: *What were some of your early experiences out in nature?*

GF: I told my parents when I was 9 that I was moving to the Rockies. I sent away money I had earned mowing lawns for a subscription to *Colorado Rocky Mountain West* magazine. I sat in the basement in South Bend and drooled over those for years. We went on a family vacation to Colorado when I was 10. After high school graduation, a friend and

BOB GROSS

I took our first backpacking trip. We had gear strapped with seatbelt webbing to our backpacks. We had Dinty Moore stew for dinner. Not exactly the poster children for backpacking, but when you're 18, you can get away with a lot. Looking back, it was a seminal trek for both of us.

Q: *What about as an adult?*

GF: I certainly loved my work for *National Geographic*'s book division on *Hawks Rest*. I walked 144 miles from my front door in Red Lodge to extreme southeast Yellowstone. I was supplied several times with items a mule train brought in. To be in that level of wilderness for that length of time was extraordinary. I've logged over 30,000 miles of trail and thousands of miles of river.

Q: *You spend so much time in the wilderness. How do you adjust to life back in town?*

GF: Red Lodge is an open friendly place. As much as I like to think of myself as independent and a loner, community is critical.

Q: *If a visitor wanted to get a sense of the true Red Lodge, not just the galleries on the main street, what would you recommend they do?*

GF: The first thing I'd do is park the car and not only walk Broadway but the neighborhoods as well. It has a wide range of abilities, talents, and socioeconomics. Go to Sam's Tap Room, go to Café Regis, of which I was a former owner, go to places like Honey's on Broadway and just sit around and talk and actually engage in the conversations of the people who are there. You'll find an openness and friendliness that perhaps you're not used to. There doesn't need to be a pre-existing relationship in place to engage with Red Lodge.

CAFÉ REGIS

JODON PHILLIPS

"If you want to be in the know, pronounce it café reh-gis," says author and former Café Regis owner Gary Ferguson. "Not ree-gis." Even if you're not hungry for fresh, organic, locally sourced food, it's worth stopping by. Before it was a cafe, the building, which dates from 1941, was in continuous operation by the Regis family as a grocery store. In fact, some of the trees and gardens behind the building are the same ones that miners bought produce from on their way to work.

The 1941 Regis Grocery is likely the only art deco building around for at least 100 miles. "I heard it was a case of function driving form," Gary says of the building's design. The family had observed "that if you angled the front door, the prevailing winds would blow it free of snow, and sure enough, that's exactly what happened," he says. *501 S. Word, (406) 446-1941, www.caferegis.com*

elevator, an elegant dining room, a unique history room, and large suites that have indoor balconies and oversized jetted tubs. A stained glass window on the east side of the building brings in the morning light. Round stained glass accent windows face out from guest suites into the gallery area. *2 North Broadway, www.thepollard.com. 406-446-0001 or 1-800-POLLARD*

⇒ Earlywood

Brad Bernhart doesn't make wooden spoons that look like spoons just because that's what they're supposed to look like. In fact, his aren't spoon-shaped at all, but flat. "It didn't take me long to realize that traditional wooden spoons are not that good at what they're supposed to do," says Brad, whose company Earlywood is based in Red Lodge.

What really got Brad thinking about an alternate design was using a traditional spoon to clean out a pan. "The traditional spoon part is round, so only one point of it makes contact with the bottom or side—you just get little squiggly marks," he says. With Earlywood's flat sauté spoon, which Brad says is Earlywood's most popular product, "you can get the whole side or bottom in one swoop."

Earlywood was featured in the food magazine *Bon Appétit* just before Christmas 2016. As a result, "We had a 3-day period where we did more sales than we did in the first 10 months of the year," Brad says. Orders on the company's website have slowed down since, but it's obviously been discovered.

LOCAL LOWDOWN
HIGH COUNTRY COWBOYS

The High Country Cowboys are an unlikely group. "We've never had any schooling musically," says John Kosel, one of three brothers in the group (Joe and Marty are the other two). "But we have a large family, and growing up, we always played one kind of music or another." There's also the fact that the brothers are rather shy. After they started singing three-part harmony and playing together in 2006, "none of us wanted to take it anywhere," John says. "We were just doing it because we liked playing and singing together."

But their older sister Theresa, the manager of Red Lodge's community center, had other ideas for them, albeit not on the scale the brothers now perform. She asked John, Joe, and Marty to perform at the community center during lunch. "We told her we guessed we could do it," John says. "We weren't so excited about it at first. I didn't think people would like the old music we do." But the High Country Cowboys were a hit and the community center wanted them to return.

Word got out about this awesome new local group and the Pollard, the historic hotel in downtown Red Lodge, asked them to play there. John recalls, "We were really hesitant about that. That *really* wasn't what we wanted to do." After their first night at the Pollard, the manager pulled the brothers aside and told them he wanted them to play there as often as they could. "That was when we decided we had better get serious about it," John says. From 2014 on, the High Country Cowboys

became a weekly fixture at the hotel. Since then, the brothers have played at Billings's Alberta Bair Theater and at that city's St. Johns Summer Concert Series and have recorded four albums.

"From our earliest album to our latest there's a big difference," John says. What hasn't changed, however, is the style of music the brothers play. "We've always been Roy Rogers fans and fans of Sons of the Pioneers. This was our dad's favorite kind of music when he was growing up. He's pretty excited how things turned out with our music."

The brothers only got into singing western harmony in 2006, after watching a DVD about learning to sing in this style by Riders in the Sky. "If Riders in the Sky could do it, we thought we could too," John says.

While they've graduated to singing some original songs, John says, "even when we write a song, it is in the style of traditional cowboy music." Marty, the youngest brother and lead singer, wrote the three original songs on the group's fourth album, *Cowboy*. (In 2015, Marty was recognized as Yodeler of the Year by the Western Music Association.)

When not on stage, the three brothers have other artistic pursuits. Guitarist John is an oil painter, bassist Joe a luthier (he made the guitars he and John play), and Marty makes leather goods from saddles to chaps. Find the brothers' schedule on their website at *www.the highcountrycowboys.com*.

COURTESY HIGH COUNTRY COWBOYS

Brad's had to hire several new staffers, but "everything is still made in Red Lodge," he says. "It's going to take a lot to make that ever change."

As much thinking as he puts into each Earlywood design, it's difficult to believe Brad started making wooden utensils as a way to relax. He was living in Bozeman and studying mechanical engineering. "I was always kind of creative, and, after 4 years of studying engineering, I was missing it," he says. The house he lived in had a lawn mower shed in the backyard. "I got a couple of simple tools, one or two pieces of wood, and started cranking away in the shed just to clear my head."

It wasn't until he was working full time as an engineer in Portland, Oregon, that Brad began thinking he could turn his hobby into a business. "I went to work during the day, and, if I wanted to relax at night, I'd go out and make a couple of spoons," he says. "About a year in, I started thinking about art fairs." Eighty percent of the designs Earlywood sells today are designs Brad came up with during his time in Portland. "I always put function ahead of fashion," he explains. "If I were to design something that I thought looked cool at the time, then I'd have to change it as time went on. But when function dictates, there is no reason to change, as long as it is designed well in the first place."

Combine Brad's timeless designs with some of the hardest woods out there, and you get wooden utensils that will be around a long time. "If a cherry spoon is around for 50 years, I wouldn't see why one of my Mexican ebony spoons wouldn't last three times as long," Brad says. All of Earlywood's utensils are made from one of four woods. The softest wood he uses is hard maple. The three harder woods are bloodwood, jotoba, and Mexican ebony. How hard are they? Well, jotoba is used to make railroad ties, just to give you an idea. *www.earlywooddesigns.com*

Festival of Nations

In its early days, when it was still a mining town, Red Lodge had residents from around the world who were mostly European immigrants. In 1951, trying to come up with a way to keep the town vital after the coal mines had closed between 1924 and 1932, officials founded the Festival of Nations. The annual, multiday ethnic festival continues to this day every August. The festival has everything from bagpipers to Celtic fusion dancers, accordion concerts, Munirah belly dancers, Scandinavian dancers, Highlands games, an ethnic potluck, readings of Roma (gypsy) folktales, and drum circles. *www.redlodge .com*

◆ ROAD TRIP 5
COOKE CITY

Cooke City–Silver Gate's small number of year-round residents and location (between Yellowstone's Northeast Entrance and Beartooth Pass) make Gardiner look like an urban transportation hub by comparison. Cooke City has one road through it, and, for 8 months of the year, the road is closed at the east end of town, making Cooke City the literal dead end. Even in summer, Cooke City takes a little work to get to, but it's worth it, whether you take the time to check out the art gallery at the town dump or not.

Cooke City Museum

Cooke City Museum is more than its name suggests. Located in the chamber of commerce building downtown, the museum tells the history of the communities of Cooke City, Silver Gate, and Colter Pass through nine permanent

GRANT ORDELHEIDE

LOCAL LOWDOWN

KELLY HARTMAN, **Curator of the Cooke City Museum**

Kelly Hartman was born on the other side of Yellowstone, in Jackson, Wyoming, but her parents moved to Cooke City before she was a year old. "When my family moved here, the one-room schoolhouse was actually closed, but it reopened right before I started to go," she says. Kelly graduated from the Cooke City School in 2003 and then went on to high school in Gardiner, Montana, 2 hours away. She later got her BFA in painting and has been the director of the Cooke City Museum since 2013 and recently moved to Bozeman to take a position as curator at the Gallatin History Museum.

Q: *How many grades were there in the school?*

KELLY HARTMAN: It was kindergarten through eighth grade.

COURTESY OF KELLY HARTMAN

Q: *And how many students at once are we talking about?*

KH: One year I was in school, we ended up having seventeen kids, and that was a lot. I had one boy that was in my grade for at least half of my schooling.

Q: *What were the logistics of class?*

KH: Each grade had its own schedule, like you would at any school. All of our desks were in one room though. The youngest kids had their own small table. There was usually a teacher's aide that would work with us in addition to the teacher. We'd work at our own pace. Maybe start with English and do however much of your assigned work you could do in that hour. If you finished, you could move onto the next thing or help other students, which was great. We'd have recess and do lots of skiing for physical education and take trips to the dump on Friday.

Q: *When you transitioned from the Cooke City School to Gardiner High School for ninth grade, how'd you do academically?*

KH: Both my younger sister, who started in Gardiner in sixth grade, and I were way ahead in reading. Academically, I was always at the top of my class. My sister was way ahead in math. I think the one-room school was great academically.

Q: *So did you ride the bus 4 hours a day to and from high school?*

KH: My parents ended up renting a house in Gardiner. We'd go up for the week. My parents own a gallery in Silver Gate, but my sister and I would stay put in Gardiner.

66

Q: *Aside from academics, how was transitioning to a bigger school?*

KH: It was very difficult. Your freshman year of high school is hard anyway and I went from having one student in my class to twenty, which isn't large by any means, but socially, I found it hard to move into a new group of people. I think my sister, because she came in a little younger, adapted a little better.

Q: *If there were just two kids in your Cooke City class, was there a graduation ceremony?*

KH: Yes. We had a valedictorian and speech and the whole community came. When I graduated, I know I was the first kid to graduate who had been to the school for all grades in 25 or 30 years. The community was always really supportive of the school.

Prior to World War I, there were an estimated 200,000 one-room schoolhouses in the United States. Today there are only around 200. Montana has about sixty one-room schoolhouses, more than any other state, but historians are worried about their future as rural residents continue to move to towns and cities. In 2013, the National Trust for Historic Preservation added Montana's one-room schoolhouses to their list of the Nation's 11 Most Endangered Historical Places. Cooke City is home to one of the state's one-room schoolhouses.

exhibits curated by lifelong resident Kelly Hartman, who also works as curator of the Gallatin History Museum. Kelly had returned to Cooke City after earning her bachelor's degree in fine arts. When the director of the museum suddenly passed away, Kelly ended up taking over and loved it. "My parents being wildlife people, we didn't learn that much about the area's mining history. I enjoyed learning about my community in a way I hadn't touched before." Since working at the Cooke City Museum, Kelly has started writing a book on the area's history between the 1870s and the 1940s.

"It's not a huge space that we have," she says, "but we have touch screens at each exhibit that can fit a lot of information." Her current favorite is a temporary exhibit that opened in 2016 and will be up for several years entitled "He Might Strike It Still." The exhibit includes letters by Anastazie Zucker, an immigrant from Bohemia and a Cooke City resident from the 1890s into the 1930s. She came to Cooke City with her miner husband, Anton, who for decades maintained the belief they would hit it big someday. They never did though. "We had some people come in and they've almost cried reading these old letters," Kelly says. "As I've learned more about Anastazie and Anton, they've become these great-great-grandparents of mine. They never struck it big enough to leave. They dug a 250-foot tunnel in their time here. I think these letters are one of the most important things we have because they tell such a story of life here." *206 W. Main St., (406) 838-2203, www.cookecitymontanamuseum.org*

Compactor Facility

It seems Silver Gate has more art galleries than homes. The most interesting art space in the area is a surprise though—it's the Cooke City Compactor facility, also known as the dump. When the facility was built in 2002, Steve Liebl was hired as manager (he was also a Realtor, caretaker, newsletter publisher, and Yellowstone firefighter). He soon began putting aside any art, books, or useable items people had thrown away. The dump became a bit of a social stop. Liebl hung the paintings and photographs on the walls inside the facility. There are now several hundred pieces of art. Steve died in 2006, but subsequent managers have kept the art collection, and also the book exchange

---

Cooke City is not technically a city. It's not even a town. Neither Cooke City nor neighboring Silver Gate are incorporated, so technically they are communities.

Steve started. The hand-painted sign urging you to recycle was painted by students at the Cooke City School including Kelly Hartman, profiled on page 66. "I can't believe it's still up there," Kelly says. "I painted that when I was in seventh or eighth grade." Kelly says out of the hundreds of paintings locals do have a favorite. "There is this one landscape with a tree and a beautiful view," she says. "I know lots of people have offered to buy it over the years, but none of the managers will sell it."

Cooke City Store

Troy Wilson started visiting Cooke City when he was 7 years old. That was in 1977. By 1984, he was working at the Cooke City Store. Beth Gould worked at the Cooke City Store for the first time in 1990. Troy and Beth got married in 1992 and went into careers in, respectively, real estate and accounting. In 2003, Troy and Beth Wilson bought the Cooke City Store. They bought it from its owners of 26 years, Ralph and Sue Glidden. The Gliddens, who had come to Cooke City from Oregon to cross-country ski for a winter, also found themselves buying the store after working at it for a couple of years.

The store was built by John Savage and John Elder on land owned by the earliest known miner in the area. It was first called Savage & Elder's. In the 1880s and 1890s, Cooke City was boom and bust—the population ranged from twenty residents to 1,000—and the general store boomed and busted with it, going through several ownership changes in the process. The name was changed to the Cooke City Store in 1906. It is one of the oldest still-operating general stores in Montana. On its centenary, it was listed on the National Register of Historic Places. While the goods on the oak shelves have changed over the store's life, the shelves themselves haven't. They're original, as is the Premiere Jr. hand-cranked cash register still used to ring up sales. *101 Main St., (406) 838-2234, cookecitystore.com*

Beartooth Café

It's doubtful the Beartooth Café has changed much since it was founded in 1979. This is a good thing. The cozy, log cafe is exactly what you'd want to find in a town with a three-block "downtown." (And the chocolate chip cookies are much better than you'd expect to find in a tiny town in the middle of nowhere.) Ownership has changed but not that often. Employees have come and gone, but current co-owner Vicki Denniston (the other two owners are Deb Purvis and Vicki's husband, Scott) says some of today's employees are the fourth generation of their family to work at the cafe.

Scott himself started as an employee before buying into the cafe with Vicki in 2007. One of Scott's friends at a small state college in West Virginia had worked at the Beartooth Café one summer and planned to go back the following summer. "The second time, I came out with him," Scott says. That was in 1997. Scott worked as a dishwasher and host. And then he came back. It was his second summer in Cooke City that he met Vicki, whose great-grandfather came to Cooke City in the 1930s. In 1998, Scott was back at the Beartooth and Vicki was working for her aunt, who owned the two buildings on either side of the cafe. "I used to watch Vicki carrying merchandise across the deck," Scott says. The two married in 2000. They now have four kids and the oldest two work full time in the cafe. "All four of them have helped out though," Vicki says. "And they love it. They tell us all the time, 'You can't sell it. We love being here.'"

The family lived full time in Cooke City until 2011, when Bobbi Dempsey, the longtime teacher at the Cooke City School, was retiring. Three of the couple's kids went to the Cooke City School. "At one point, there were six kids in the school and three of them were mine," Vicki says. "With Bobbi retiring and Mikayla going to be in the fifth grade, we thought it was time to move to Livingston." Scott says, "Winters in Cooke City are beautiful and really special—a friend and I had a tradition of going out and getting Christmas trees together—but they are a lot of work. You have to deal with the elements. You're shoveling constantly." Vicki says, "In a bad year, spring won't come to

Cooke City until July. In a good year, you can have some nice warmups in April and May you can see a few flowers blooming."

The Beartooth Café is open every day between late May and late September and the Dennistons live in Cooke City all summer. "I like to think it's a staple in the community," Vicki says. "We've kept everything as consistent as possible. The owner Scott worked for had some great recipes—people really like the lasagna—and we kept most of them. People who ate here 30 years ago come back now and it is almost the exact same."

One thing that has changed is the demographics of the cafe's thirty seasonal staffers. "We have kids now come from all over the world to work here," Vicki says. "Last year we had two girls from China, two kids from the Czech Republic, a boy from Romania, one from Turkey, and college students from all over the US. We've even had college professors that have worked for us dishwashing. People just want to be here in the summer. It's fun."

FYI: The cafe bakes four different kinds of cookies—chocolate chip, peanut butter, ginger snap, and oatmeal raisin—fresh every morning. Vicki warns that they sell out fast. *14 Main St., (406) 838-2475, www.beartoothcafe.com*

BEARTOOTH CAFÉ

ROAD TRIP 6
HIGH COUNTRY

The interesting geology doesn't end at the borders of Yellowstone National Park. No areas show this more than the Beartooth and Absaroka (pronounced ab-ZORE-ka) mountains on the park's northeast border. Much of the two ranges are protected by the 943,648-acre Beartooth-Absaroka Wilderness, which was created in 1978. Though these ranges are neighbors, they are very different. The Absarokas are composed of volcanic and metamorphic rock, while the Beartooths are granitic with some rocks dated to be 4 billion years old, making them some of the oldest exposed rocks on the planet. The Beartooths are also considered the most biologically unique mountain range in the country, have twenty-five peaks higher than 12,000 feet, and include the largest high-elevation plateau in the Lower 48 states.

↓ Top of the World

If you're pedaling your road bike from Cooke City to Red Lodge via the Beartooth Highway, which hundreds of cyclists do every summer because it's one of the country's classic alpine rides, you'll be disappointed when you

COURTESY TOP OF THE WORLD

LOCAL LOWDOWN

BEN ZAVORA, Founder of Beartooth Powder Guides

The mountains around Cooke City often have more snow than anywhere else in the Lower 48 states. Snowmobilers realized this a long time ago; skiers have only recently become aware of this. The opening of Beartooth Powder Guides (BPG) in late 2012 by Ben Zavora is spreading the news. BPG not only does guided ski outings, but also has a backcountry log cabin and yurt you can rent for the night. Ben's permit from the Forest Service requires the yurt be taken down each spring, but the cabin is available to rent year-round. When the snow finally melts, it's a great base camp for hiking in the Beartooth mountains. *(406) 838-2097, beartoothpowder.com*

Q: *Where did the idea of opening a ski guiding company in Cooke City come from?*

BEN ZAVORA: I lived in Bozeman for 15 years and had skied in the backcountry around Cooke City a few times every winter. And then I had a life change where I had to start from scratch. I decided to restart in Cooke City and rebuild with my dream business.

Q: *Did you grow up skiing?*

BZ: I grew up in Encinitas, California, and was always into skiing and the mountains more than the beach. I'd ski at Mammoth. I eventually decided to become a ski bum and moved to Squaw Valley. There I met a fellow who is still one of my best friends. The following winter he moved to Bozeman. He called and told me he found the best spot to be a powder skier. I moved to Bozeman in the fall of 1996.

Q: *The BPG office in Cooke City is across the street from Bearclaw Bakery. Is that dangerous?*

BZ: Super dangerous. I stopped and got two pieces of carrot cake this morning.

Q: *How many days a year do you ski?*

BZ: It depends on the time of year. November tends to be a lot of chores—working on getting firewood for the cabin and yurt and stuff. December and January, I'm doing my avalanche education season, so I'm out teaching 3 or 4 days a week for 2 months. February, March, and April is our peak guiding season; that's when I'm out the most.

COURTESY OF BEN ZAVORA

Q: *How are the yurt and cabin different?*

BZ: They're only 10 miles apart as the crow flies, but they are completely different geologically. The terrain around the yurt—you're right at alpine level, at 9,500 feet—it's granite and big alpine terrain. At the cabin, you're in the healthiest whitebark pine forest in the Greater Yellowstone Ecosystem. It's great tree skiing.

Q: *Do you have a favorite between the two?*

BZ: The cabin is very dear to my heart because I built it, but they are so different. My favorite would be the cabin for December, January, and February and the summer and the yurt for March and April.

Q: *When you say you built the cabin, are you being literal?*

BZ: Yes. I logged it all by hand right off the property—standing dead timber. It's in an area where no motors are allowed, so I had to do everything by hand. It was hard work, but I still say it was the most fun 4 months of my life.

Skiing is only part of being a good backcountry skier. Because backcountry skiing is done in areas where there is no ski patrol mitigating avalanche conditions, backcountry skiers must educate themselves about traveling safely in terrain that can be dangerous. BPG runs Beartooth Powder University to help skiers learn to do this.

get to the Top of the World Resort. Everyone else traveling by car on this scenic highway will greet the Top of the World with a smile. Why these different reactions? Coming from the west, the Top of the World Resort is still 1,500 feet below the top of the climb that culminates in crossing the Beartooth Pass. So, for cyclists, it's a cruel joke.

The Top of the World Store, which sells cold drinks, ice cream, and candy bars in what feels like the middle of nowhere, predates the completion of the Beartooth Highway. The store opened directly across from the boat ramp for Beartooth Lake in 1932. (The highway opened in 1936.) In the early 1960s, the Forest Service—it's in the Shoshone National Forest—wanted the store to move. That happened at the end of the 1964 season. Since then, the store has been about halfway between Island and Beartooth Lakes. At its present location, the enterprise was able to grow. There is now a campground and modest motel—it has four rooms—in addition to the store. You can rent canoes and paddleboats and fishing rods, both for spin casting and fly fishing.

Because the resort is surrounded by creeks and tarns—which you can fish in after getting the required permits—in July the mosquitoes are fierce. *2823 Hwy. 212, (307) 587-5368, topoftheworldresort.com*

Beartooth Highway

The Beartooth Highway, which connects Cooke City with Red Lodge, Montana, passes through terrain no sensible road should. For an entire 10 miles, it is above 10,000 feet. (Its entire length is 68 miles.) It is the highest-elevation highway in Wyoming and Montana and in the northern Rockies. The late CBS correspondent Charles Kuralt pronounced the road "the most beautiful drive in America." You'll see a waterfall, too many high alpine lakes to count, snowfields, glaciers, the Beartooth Wilderness, and boulder fields. You could spot grizzly and black bears, moose, bighorn sheep, Rocky Mountain goats, elk, or a mountain lion. Between Cooke City and Red Lodge, the highway climbs and descends more than 6,000 feet.

Built between 1931 and 1936, the Beartooth Highway was one of the first ten roads in the country to be designed a National Scenic Byways All-American Road, the highest honor related to scenery any road can get. (This happened in 2002.) You can't get this level of beauty without some drawbacks though. The biggest one? It's only open about 5 months of the year. The Beartooth Mountains get about 30 feet of snow every winter—too much for snowplows to deal with—and the highway crosses numerous avalanche paths. So even if the snowplows could keep up, it's too dangerous for them to be in the area. It opens the Saturday of Memorial Day weekend (in May) and closes the Tuesday after Columbus Day (in October).

Even when it's open, chances are snowplows will have to do some work at its higher elevations. It has snowed at the summit of Beartooth Pass–10,987 feet–every month of the year. There is often a 30-degree temperature difference between Cooke City or Red Lodge and the top of the pass. The highway is also in danger from mudslides. In the spring of 2005, multiple mudslides destroyed about 12 miles of the highway on the eastern side of the pass. It cost $20 million to fix the road and took months. The repair work was finished only a few days before the road closed for the winter.

Drivers who have a fear of heights need to steel themselves if they take this route. There are several instances where switchbacks cling to the side of a mountain and you can look down a couple of thousand feet. There are also instances of the opposite: where rock walls overhang the road and it's so tight you can reach out and touch them. *Mdt.mt.gov/travinfo/beartooth*

↓ Biking the Beartooth Highway

However you define an "epic" bike ride–views, difficulty, weather, terrain, mosquitos–the Beartooth Highway exceeds it. The ride between Cooke City and Red Lodge, Montana, is 68 miles. Over this distance, you climb 5,000 or 6,000 feet. (Cooke City has a higher starting elevation than Red Lodge, so there's less climbing riding east.)

GRANT ORDELHEIDE

The Beartooth Highway passes through terrain no sensible road should.
ADOBE STOCK

On both sides, the climbing is spread over about 25 miles, so it is never terribly steep. There might be a section that's 7 degrees in pitch, but nothing steeper. Ten miles in the middle undulate between 10,000 feet and 10,987 feet. Since tree line in this area is about 9,000 feet, there is nowhere to hide. Bring warm gloves and a hat to put on under your helmet.

While this road is an engineering marvel, it was not constructed with cyclists in mind. When there is a shoulder, it is no more than 3 feet wide. This isn't as disconcerting as it usually is on highways because the speed limit is slow, and the road's twists, turns, and the surrounding scenery force drivers to stick to it. When it comes time for the descent, chances are cyclists will pass cars; bikes can handle the turns at higher speeds.

This is also an epic ride for motorcyclists. Annually in mid-July, bikers come from across the country for the 3-day Beartooth Rally. *(406) 425-7397, beartoothrally.com*

Beartooth Basin Summer Ski Area

Just below the top of Beartooth Pass is the only ski area in the country that's open for summer and not winter. Its season starts Memorial Day weekend and ends July 4 . . . snow conditions permitting. In 2015 and 2016, snow conditions did not permit. "All we need is an average winter," says Justin Modroo, one of the resort's five owners. "But we rarely have an average winter." Justin says the owners flew over the ski area in April 2016. "Just looking, you can tell how much snow there is; how much of the snow towers are covered? We could see rocks in our lift line course." Beartooth Basin's parking lot is at 10,900 feet. The bottom of its two ski lifts are 1,000 feet below.

Beartooth Basin was founded in the 1960s by three Austrian ski coaches as the Red Lodge International Ski Camp. It was only open to private groups. "The whole thing was put in to have a training area for Olympic athletes," Justin says. It wasn't until the late 1990s, when some of the current owners first bought into the ski area, that it was opened to the public. In 2003, the name was changed to Beartooth Basin Summer Ski Area.

Although the ski area is only 600 acres, less than one-quarter the size of Jackson Hole Mountain Resort 100+ miles to the south, "you can get puckered up and it feels like you're really getting after it," Justin says. This is because all of the ski runs are below a big cornice. To ski them, you have to get past the cornice. "The easiest way in, it's 30 or 40 degrees," Justin says. "You can launch right off the cornice; then it's 90 degrees. The terrain we offer is pretty advanced." There isn't a single beginner run. Neither is there a lodge. Bathrooms are port-a-potties and lift tickets and snacks are sold out of an RV. *23 miles south of Red Lodge on Hwy. 212, Beartoothbasin.com*

LOCAL LOWDOWN

JUSTIN MODROO, Owner of Beartooth Basin
Summer Ski Area

Justin Modroo grew up in Billings and ski racing at Red Lodge Mountain. In the early 2000s, he competed in the World Free-Skiing Tour, which holds big mountain skiing competitions around the world. Twice Justin finished in the Top 10 overall. While he was competing, he also earned bachelor's and master's degrees in geophysics. He bought into the ski area "in about 2012," he says. "I knew it was a good opportunity and I knew they could use the help. It's definitely a labor of love," Justin says. "We're not really making any money and any money we do make we tend to throw back into equipment."

Austin Hart is the president of the owners' group and Justin is the vice president. "We're basically the operators as well," he says. "Usually between Austin and myself, one of us is up there every day. Kurt Hallock [another owner] comes up too." Justin says that on any given day, there are only five employees working. "Because we have such a small staff, most everyone can do multiple things. They'll bounce around for the day, and that's what Austin and I do too when we're up there. We'll go and fill one of the lifties for a while, or work the ticket booth."

BEARTOOTH BASIN

Red Lodge Mountain

The origins of Red Lodge Mountain ski resort are in two rope tows and a 500-vertical-foot drop at the base of Grizzly Peak in the early 1950s. The Silver Run Ski Club, which had several hundred members who lived in Red Lodge, Billings, and nearby towns, cut two runs and installed two rope tows and the Willow Creek Ski Area was born. One rope tow served beginner terrain while the other took skiers to steeper runs in the trees.

By 1952, club members admitted Willow Creek had some problems, including car-sized sagebrush in the middle of runs and a lack of snow. A "run" could often only be done by piecing together various snow patches. They went looking for somewhere else to put in runs and lifts. The main requirements were varied terrain and more snow. They found it up on Grizzly Peak. Well, kind of.

Grizzly Peak opened in 1960 with wonderfully varied terrain. (It was several years later the name was changed to Red Lodge Mountain.) Ski club

members had only spent time exploring it in the spring though. They soon learned the area didn't get much late-fall to early-winter snow. The big storms runs needed for coverage often don't come until January and February. Some years, the resort hasn't been able to open until January. While this was a problem for business in the early years—there was the winter the resort's finances were so tight it couldn't afford to hire lifties and Red Lodge business owners came together to get the lifts staffed for free all season—the resort is doing just fine now with one of the best snow-making systems in the state.

Still, Red Lodge Mountain is not a ski resort you fly to, and it doesn't want to be. "It is very much a locals' resort," says Jeff Carroll, director of sales and marketing at the resort since 2009. "We like to position it as non-fancy. We value a good ski experience over glitz or glamour and crowds." Jeff admits that during winter holidays, you might find a line at one of the two high-speed detachable quad lifts. "You might have to wait 5 minutes," he says. *305 Ski Run Rd., (800) 444-8977, Redlodgemountain.com*

RED LODGE MOUNTAIN, KELSEY BORGE

Sylvan Peak Mountain Shop

Mary Ellen Mangus opened Sylvan Peak on Red Lodge's main street in 1990. Today the shop sells everything you could ever need to hike, climb, or ski in the backcountry, but when it opened, it sold only clothing. And all of the clothing was designed and sewn by Mary Ellen herself. Mary Ellen named her brand and shop after the nearby mountain of the same name. The mountain called Sylvan Peak is one of the first peaks you see when driving into the East Rosebud drainage west of Red Lodge in the Beartooth Mountains. You can hike to the peak's 11,935-foot summit, and the views from it are worth the effort, but it's more popular with rock climbers than hikers.

Mary Ellen made, and still makes, kids clothing and fleece jackets and vests. At one point, she employed six or seven seamstresses but today does all of the sewing herself. "She took a 2-year hiatus and then figured out she loved it and now she's back [at age 78]," says her daughter, Marci, who now runs the shop with her husband, Mike. "Everything Sylvan Peak today is something she made." Marci says that when locals heard Mary Ellen was sewing again they started "bringing in 15-year-old pants, or their favorite jacket asking if she can make them another one."

Marci says Sylvan Peak's current designs are the same ones her mom made in the 1990s. "Some of the designs from 26 years ago are pretty epic." Marci says all of the designs are "kind of my favorite," but admits that the "hot ticket item" is the baby booties. "I remember having hand-me-down bags of kids clothing that I gave to friends, and they always asked if there were some of mom's booties in there." When asked if she sews, Marci says, "I didn't get that good, creative gene from her. I can sew effectively, but it's not pretty."

In addition to selling gear from Mary Ellen's fleece vests to sleeping bags and backpacks, Sylvan Peak happily gives trail recommendations. "I have one person on staff in the summer that that is all they do—get people set up with a hike," Marci says. Some of her favorite trails close to town are the Lake Fork of Rock Creek and the West Fork of Rock Creek. "Both wander along Rock Creek, and, depending how far in you get, there are lakes and waterfalls. Depending on the time of year, there are nice flowers." *9 S. Broadway, (406) 446-1770, www.sylvanpeak.com*

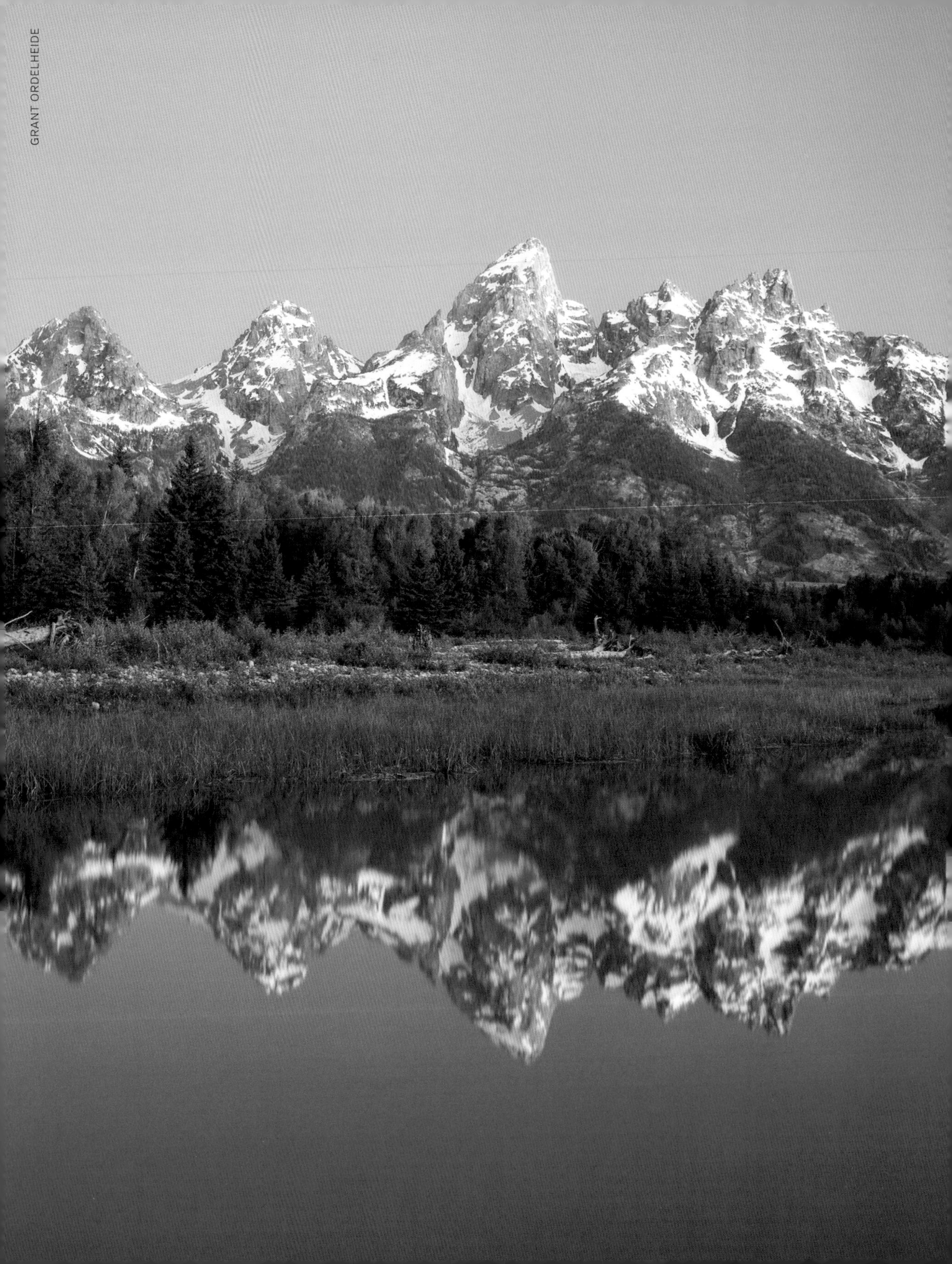

GRANT ORDELHEIDE

Leaving the South Entrance of Yellowstone puts you at the north end of the valley known as Jackson Hole. This 40-or-so-mile-long valley figures in more dreams about America's Wild West than perhaps anywhere else. Unlike many dreams though, Jackson Hole stands the test of reality. At the Million Dollar Cowboy Bar in Jackson (the only incorporated town in the valley and also the valley's largest community), "stools" are western saddles rather than traditional seats. Sidewalks in downtown Jackson are wood rather than cement. In the winter, about 6,000 to 7,000 elk migrate down from the surrounding mountains to the National Elk Refuge, which is immediately adjacent to downtown Jackson. The human population of Jackson isn't much more than 8,000.

And then there is the scenery, which is just as wild as the climate and the resident cowboys. "These are what mountains are supposed to look like," said American president Teddy Roosevelt the first time he saw the Teton mountain range. Erupting 7,000 feet from the valley floor with not so much as a foothill to temper their rise, the Tetons are the youngest range in the Rockies. Toothy and glaciated, they're the centerpiece of Grand Teton National Park and draw photographers, skiers, and climbers from around the world. Some visitors decide to stay.

But the Tetons aren't Jackson Hole's only mountains. The valley is ringed by mountains—the Gros Ventre Mountains, the Snake River Range, the Absarokas, and the Wyoming Range. This makes the area difficult to get to—driving into the valley from Yellowstone is the easiest drive, actually. The nearest highway with more than one lane in each direction is about 100 miles away. Two of the four roads out of the valley require driving over steep mountain passes. The nearest metropolitan area with a population of over 1 million is a 5-hour drive. If you fly here, enjoy the novelty of landing at Jackson Hole Airport, the only airport in the country inside a national park.

Because of its beauty and amenities, Jackson Hole has long been a playground for the rich and famous who don't want to flaunt their riches or fame. Harrison Ford lives quietly on a ranch here, and former vice president Dick Cheney does the same (just on a golf course rather than a ranch). No one is surprised if they see Sandra Bullock, Jim Carrey, Sting, Robert Downey Jr., or Brad Pitt strolling along Jackson's wooden boardwalks or enjoying wine and pizza on the deck of Dornans in Moose. Yes, there is a community in Jackson Hole called Moose. And yes, you can often spot moose there.

◆ ROAD TRIP 1
KELLY

Bison sometimes outnumber people in Kelly, an island of private land on the banks of the Gros Ventre River and entirely surrounded by Grand Teton National Park. The community's human population is about 200. The Jackson Hole bison herd is between 500 and 700 animals. Still Kelly has its own school and post office and, arguably, the valley's best espresso. In the 1920s, Kelly was in the running against Jackson to become the county seat, but in May 1927, it was destroyed by a flash flood resulting from the collapse of the natural dam formed across the Gros Ventre River 2 years earlier during a massive landslide.

→ Mormon Row and Moulton Barn

During Mormon Row's heyday—the late 1880s and the first couple of decades of the 1900s—there were as many as twenty-seven homesteads, all belonging to families in the Church of Latter Day Saints. There was a school and a

church. And, at the time, the area wasn't called Mormon Row, but Grovont. It was a Norman Rockwell–esque community. Barn raisings were giant affairs. In the winter, kids skated on frozen irrigation ditches and sled on Blacktail Butte. In the summer, families picked huckleberries around Taggart Lake and community picnics were a big deal.

The last families moved away from Mormon Row in the early 1960s, shortly after the surrounding area became part of Grand Teton National Park. Only six homesteads still stand today. The most famous of the surviving homesteads is that of Thomas Alma Moulton. A barn he built between 1913 and 1938 is quite possibly the most photographed barn in the country, perhaps even the world. Images of the T. A. Moulton Barn have appeared on billboards in Times Square, jigsaw puzzles around the world, and above the deli in Jackson's Albertsons. In 1997, Mormon Row and the T. A. Moulton Barn were listed in the National Register of Historic Places for their importance both to vernacular architecture and local history.

Jackson Hole Bison Herd

Like most of North America, Jackson Hole was historically home to bison. No one is sure how many bison lived on the continent prior to Columbus's arrival, but experts guesstimate there could have been as many as 60 million. North America's bison herds were the largest community of wild animals ever to walk the earth. By the end of the 19th century, however, they had been hunted to near extinction and only about 800 animals remained. But bison were never made extinct in the Greater Yellowstone Ecosystem (GYE). The GYE is the only place in North America an endemic population of wild bison has lived since prehistoric times.

While bison were not fully exterminated in Yellowstone, it was a different story in Jackson Hole. Jackson Hole was bison free from the late 1800s until 1948. That year, twenty bison from the Yellowstone herd were installed on a 1,500-acre wildlife refuge near Moran. The herd was kept on the refuge until they escaped on their own in 1968. At that point, the "herd" contained only eleven animals. The next year, wildlife officials decided to let the bison roam free. Today the herd is about 500–700 bison and is one of the largest free-ranging herds in the country. (The largest free-ranging herd of bison in the country is the Yellowstone herd, which numbers about 4,000–5,000 bison.)

The largest mammals in North America, bison can run upwards of 30 miles per hour and jump a 6-foot fence. Males weigh up to 2,000 pounds and stand about 6 feet tall.

The sage flats south of Moran and also around Mormon Row and Kelly are some of the surest spots to see some of Jackson Hole's bison. (In the winter, the bison migrate onto the National Elk Refuge and often hang out in places people can't visit.)

→ Gros Ventre Slide

It's been more than 90 years since the north slope of Sheep Mountain, also known as Sleeping Indian, collapsed, but the scar is still fresh enough to be seen from miles away. On June 23, 1925, this landslide, which was one of the largest and fastest in the world, happened just east of Kelly. In just 3 minutes, 50 million cubic yards of rock, soil, and other debris slid down from an altitude of 9,000 feet. (This is enough debris to cover the entirety of Washington, DC, 6 inches deep.) The state surveyor at the time, W. O. Owen, estimated that, had they been able to move earth at the speed of the Gros Ventre Slide, the builders of the Panama Canal could have dug the canal in 54 minutes.

Debris made it all the way to the bottom of the mountain, dammed the Gros Ventre River, and continued 400 feet up the opposite slope. The dam across the Gros Ventre River was 2,000 feet wide, a mile long, and 225 to 250 feet high. Behind this dam a new lake formed and was named Lower Slide Lake. It was 5 miles long.

Although engineers, geologists, and various scientists pronounced this natural dam safe, it collapsed in May 1927 and flooded Kelly, killing six people and causing massive property damage. The floodwaters were massive enough to even wet Jackson's streets, 12 miles away.

Despite the collapse of the natural dam, Lower Slide Lake still exists today, although much reduced in size. It is popular for stand-up paddleboarding. The Gros Ventre Slide has been recognized as a National Geologic Site. The slide is best viewed from the Gros Ventre Road.

LOCAL LOWDOWN
WENDELL LOCKE FIELD, Painter

Wendell Locke Field grew up drawing and painting, but, when it was time for him to pick a college major, his parents' sensibility prevailed and he got a degree in agricultural business instead of art. "They didn't want me to starve," he says. Since graduating from the University of Wyoming in 1987, Field has painted continuously. He hasn't done a thing related to agricultural business, although living in a yurt in Kelly since 2006, he's been pretty close to animals, albeit wild ones rather than stock.

One winter night, Wendell was in bed inside his yurt, where his headboard was up against the exterior wall. As Wendell lay there, he heard a bison breathing and "could feel the expansion and contraction of his breath through the wall." Wendell didn't sleep at all that night. At first light, he poked his head out his door to see exactly how close the bison was. "He was leaning against the yurt exactly where my bed was. It was the coolest thing. It energized me so much for the whole next week."

Interestingly, Wendell rarely puts wildlife into his paintings. More usual are signs of human presence. Kelly's yurts are a favorite subject. "Kelly itself is soulful and authentic and its buildings feel like they belong and are in harmony with the environment," he says.

To find the essence of his art, for a period Wendell stopped seriously looking at the work of other artists. "I wanted to see what my art was without the influence of others," he says. Wendell thinks this period was successful and that, "at the end, the art was more me." Wendell is very much like Kelly then: soulful and authentic. *www.wendellfield.com*

KELLY YURT PARK

Yurts—called *gers* by the Mongolian nomads that invented them—have been around for thousands of years. They are circular tent-like homes that have about 450 square feet of living space. There's been a small community of them in Kelly since 1981. The thirteen in Kelly are made from all-weather vinyl fabric, while those on the steppes of Mongolia and Kyrgyzstan are made of wool or animal skin. While Central Asians still move their yurts seasonally, the yurts in Kelly are stationary. Kelly yurts have power, but no running water. The yurt park residents share a bathhouse. And while it's called the Kelly Yurt Park, it's not a public park, so please don't go walking through their front yards, or wander into the bathhouse.

NICK COTE

Gros Ventre Road

The Gros Ventre Road starts with a natural warm springs. Go ahead and stop for a soak–you can't miss it. The pond is 20 feet off the road–and then the road heads east, winding deep into the Gros Ventre Mountains. It's arguably one of the most beautiful drives in the valley–passing through a mix of public (Bridger-Teton National Forest) and private land (historic ranches). Most of the time, it parallels the Gros Ventre River. Sometimes the road is at river level. Other times, it hangs several hundred feet above, carved into the side of a butte. (Warning: This road does not have guardrails.)

At its beginning, this road is paved. Within several miles though, it deteriorates–expect sizeable potholes and wash-board in the dirt–but its condition is not so bad that a regular passenger car can't handle it, at least until the bridge over Crystal Creek, about 10 miles east of the warm springs. You'll pass Upper Slide and Lower Slide Lakes, which were both formed nearly a century ago by the massive Gros Ventre Slide and both of which you'll want to stop at. This road also passes the aptly named Red Hills. In early summer, the bright green fields of the ranches at the base of these hills, which live up to their name, provide for stunning photos. (These guest ranches are only open to visitors who have made advance reservations.) If you want to do some exploring on foot, several unimproved campgrounds, a boat launch, and trailheads are off this road. You could drive all the way to Cora, Wyoming, but eventually the road becomes a two-track best ridden on a dirt bike. The Crystal Creek bridge is a nice turnaround spot. The return drive has great Teton views.

→ Blacktail Butte

Sitting directly across from the Moose entrance to Grand Teton National Park, Blacktail Butte doesn't look like much, at least when compared to the Tetons. Whereas the Grand Teton's summit is sharp-edged, obvious, and 13,775 feet tall, Blacktail Butte's summit is nebulous and a mere 7,688 feet tall. Hidden on this butte's southeast flanks is a short-but-steep hike (if you've got knee issues, this might not be the hike for you) that offers some of the best views of the Tetons in the valley.

Blacktail Butte is in Grand Teton National Park, but, unlike most of the park's other trails, it is not marked. Nor is it on any maps. It is easy to find nevertheless.

From the Gros Ventre Road, about 1.5 miles west of Kelly, turn onto Mormon Row Road. The turn is just east of the Gros Ventre Campground. About ⅓ mile up Mormon Row Road, there's a large parking area to the west. Park here. The trail snakes up the ridge immediately in front of you.

In May and early June, you can catch primrose in bloom at the base of the butte, then lupine, sticky geranium, and Indian paintbrush a little higher, and finally arrowleaf balsam root around the top.

The bottom ¾ mile are the steepest. After climbing up about 800 feet over 2 miles, you emerge onto a ridge with nothing between it and the Tetons. Trees to the north prevent 360-degree views, but you can still see Sleeping Indian, Jackson Peak, downtown Jackson, Snow King, South Park, the Snake River Range, Mt. Glory, Jackson Hole Mountain Resort, Buck, the Grand, Owen, Teewinot, and Moran.

Kelly on the Gros Ventre

Al and Heather Hunter, the 40-somethings who have been running the Kelly on the Gros Ventre store since 2010, are always ready to chat about the local bison herd, the talk of the town, or espresso, which is made here on a machine custom built in Florence, Italy. Al, a former wine guy, has turned his taste buds to espresso since Kelly on the Gros Ventre (KGV) can't sell wine. His "Yurtian" (pronounced like Martian), a regular coffee amped up with an espresso shot, honors Kelly's community of yurts. The shop also sells soft drinks, sandwiches, and snacks, and firewood "by the hug," with payment accepted on the honor system.

◆ ROAD TRIP 2
THE WEST BANK

On the west bank of the Snake River, things are a little quieter, although not in winter when the Jackson Hole Mountain Resort (JHMR) uses bombs to do avalanche control on its ski slopes. Only a 15-minute drive from downtown Jackson, the communities of Wilson and Teton Village feel like another world, and make Jackson look like a metropolis. Wilson might have only 1,000 year-round residents. Teton Village is even smaller.

R Park

Fishing, floating, or swimming in one of the three ponds at R Park just past the Wyoming 22 bridge over the Snake River, you'd be hard pressed to guess the area was a working gravel pit for 20 years. If the original reclamation plan for the 40 acres—a developer wanted to divide it into three parcels and build an 8,000-square-foot spec home on each—had happened, it's possible the site would still have three ponds, one for each house. You certainly wouldn't be able to swim or fish in any of them though, at least not without getting arrested for trespassing. If the developer had had his way, you'd also be denied a walk along the site's 1,000 feet of Snake River frontage.

But luckily none of this happened. In 2011, local conservation groups purchased the 40 acres from the developer, and, because their goal was to turn it into a public park, they set about seeking community input on a design and the amenities it should have. The rehabilitation of the land and completion of the park took 5 years.

In addition to the ponds, which aren't just swimming holes for people, but important habitat for wildlife like swans, geese, osprey, porcupine, and moose, the park has five play berms. These are in lieu of artificial play structures. "Studies show that children not only need more time outdoors and in nature, but also need that time to be less structured and less scheduled," says Elizabeth Rohrbach, the park's director of development and communications. In winter, the berms offer some of the best sledding around. In summer, they're sites of old-fashioned King of the Hill games. *rendezvous landsconservancy.org*

The Snake River is the fourth-largest river in the United States.
DEPOSIT PHOTOS

LOCAL LOWDOWN
CONNIE KEMMERER, Owner Jackson Hole Mountain Resort

One of the owners (with brother Jay and sister Betty) of Jackson Hole Mountain Resort since 1992, Connie Kemmerer grew up ice-skating, not skiing. The first time she took the tram to the 10,450-foot summit of Rendezvous Mountain she was in her 20s and her family didn't yet own the resort. "It was such a huge experience to get to the top of a mountain like that; I was blown away," she says. "And then I was grateful to make it down the mountain alive. I really wasn't a very good skier." Connie did learn to ski after she had kids. "I learned to ski alongside them." By the time her family bought the resort, she says, "I was a good enough skier to ski the mountain, but still had plenty to learn."

Q: *Such as?*

CONNIE KEMMERER: I trained with an instructor to ski Corbet's (a double black diamond ski run that requires a 10-foot jump at the very beginning). I was determined to do it. I think I'm the oldest person to go into Corbet's three times in a row.

Q: *Why'd you do it three times in a row?*

CK: To see if it would diminish the fear of it.

Q: *Did it work?*

CK: No. It's always scary. Also, jumping in the second time, I hit the wall and my skis fell off before I ever hit the ground. Afterwards, [world extreme ski champion] Doug Coombs,

who was climbing nearby, told me I only missed making the turn by an inch. Of course, after that I had to go again, it was like getting back on a horse.

Q: *Favorite places to ski?*

CK: I like to ski off the tram, the gondola, and Teton lift, but as long as I'm skiing on the resort, I have a feeling of responsibility. I like skiing in the backcountry because there I feel free. Four Shadows is probably my favorite run anywhere around the resort. You get the adventure of hiking up [Cody] Peak and then it's always scary to jump in over the cornice.

Q: *Who's the better skier—you or Jay?*

CK: Me! I'm more of a daredevil. I've always felt more at home in the mountains and doing sports, adventuring, than around people. I'm sort of shy around people.

For 5 years after its 1966 opening, Jackson Hole Mountain Resort sold lifetime ski passes. One hundred and thirty people bought them. When the resort celebrated its fiftieth anniversary in 2016, 60 of these passes were still in use. *Jacksonhole.com*

Via Ferrata

The Tetons are the birthplace of American alpinism, and Teton climbs and summits continue to draw alpinists from around the world to the valley. It is partially because of this history (and partially because JHMR co-owner Connie Kemmerer is herself an alpinist) that the Tetons are home to the first *via ferrata* on any US public land. Italian for "iron road," a via ferrata is an aided, protected climbing route. There are iron rungs drilled into and affixed to the rock and also a steel cable running alongside the route so that climbers can clip into them to prevent falls. There are several *via ferrate* at the top of the Bridger Gondola at JHMR, in the Bridger-Teton National Forest.

Because it doesn't require the level of skill rock climbing does, a via ferrata allows inexperienced alpinists the opportunity to try the sport. These via ferrate have the additional benefit of being at the top of the gondola, so no uphill hiking is required to get to them, although none of the via ferrate at JHMR are accessible to anyone who's afraid of heights. Near the end of one "beginner" via ferrata, there's a 123-foot-long, 24-inch-wide suspension

bridge as high as 80 feet off the ground. The via ferrate rated intermediate and advanced take you up to a prow with serious exposure. While there are additional hand and foot holds, these routes feel as exposed as the golden staircase pitch on the Upper Exum climbing route on the Grand Teton. *Jacksonhole.com*

Teton Pass

At 8,431 feet, Teton Pass is a rare weakness in the toothy, 45-mile-long Teton Range. Native Americans were the first to find and use it to cross between the valleys on either side of the mountains, but, of course, Teton Pass wasn't official until fur trader and explorer Wilson Price Hunt "discovered" it in 1811 while on his way to the West Coast. He had previously scouted the Snake River as a route out of the valley, but thought its rapids "mad." Hunt deemed going up and over Teton Pass easier. He was right. The pass is still the most direct route into and out of the valley.

The first road over Teton Pass opened in 1918, but it wasn't until 1938 that it was plowed in winter. The current highway opened in 1969. Today thousands of commuters drive over the pass daily—many people who work in Jackson Hole live in Teton Valley, Idaho . . . and hundreds of people ski it.

NIKITA MAMOCHINE

Jackson Hole Mountain Resort is only 20 minutes northeast of Teton Pass and is often rated as one of the best ski resorts in the country. But the skiers and snowboarders who play on Teton Pass are of a different sort: They don't use lifts. Teton Pass is the heart of Jackson Hole's backcountry ski scene. Here, any day between late October and May, you can stop in the parking lot at the top and watch athletes strap skis and snowboards to their backs and hike 1,800 feet straight up Mt. Glory on the north side of the pass. Once at the top, they'll step into their skis or boards and choose from dozens of different lines down.

Skiers go to the south side of the pass too, but in this area, they use specialized boots and bindings and affix climbing skins to the bottoms of their skis rather than hike. It's the same as Mt. Glory in that they have to climb to the top of any line under their own power before they can ski it. The reason for all of this work? Fresh powder.

While Teton Pass might be one of the country's most easily accessed backcountry areas, this fact does not diminish the danger of backcountry skiing. Avalanches happen and people have died in them while skiing around Teton Pass. Several local groups offer various levels of avalanche safety classes. Classes are multiday and include classroom time and lessons in the field. *jhavalanche.org*

LOCAL LOWDOWN
ANDY AND KICHAN OLPIN, Owners of
Wilson Backcountry Sports

Jackson Hole has more gear shops than you could visit in a week, but only one is at the base of Teton Pass: Wilson Backcountry Sports. Andy and Kichan (kee-shan) Olpin opened their shop in 1993, and you can still see them there almost every day (except Sundays, when it's closed, and in the spring and fall off-seasons when the store is open but Andy and Kichan are off mountain biking in Moab).

The couple, who met dancing at the Mangy Moose Saloon (one of the original bars in Teton Village), still gets out skiing 2 to 3 days a week. Of course when they ski, they ski the back-country. From Wilson Backcountry Sports's front door, you can be at the top of the pass in 10 minutes.

When asked what are their favorite pieces of gear, Andy responds, "Our bikes and our skis."

When asked for a good half-day ski itinerary for someone new to Teton Pass, Andy says, "It depends on the individual—we try to suggest appropriate tours for what the skier is look-ing for and what is right for their ability and skill set. But for the first time on the pass, it is always good to check out Edelweiss [a low-level incline slope] and get the lay of the land and Edelweiss is usually a safe option." You should never head anywhere in the backcoun-try on skis, snowboard, or snowshoes with-out the proper equipment and training. *wilson backcountry.com*

NIKITA MAMOCHINE

Walk or bike up the original road over Teton Pass—it's closed to motorized vehicles—and you'll see that today's route is a superhighway. This first road over Teton Pass opened in July 1918 but wasn't plowed in winter until 1938. This road was the only way to get over Teton Pass until the current highway opened in 1969. Since the new highway opened, the original road was renamed Old Pass Road and is a favorite with locals seeking a quick nature fix. Crater Lake is just over 1 mile from and about 500 vertical feet above the Trail Creek trailhead and has a lovely bench to take a rest on.

NIKITA MAMOCHINE

↑ Hungry Jack's General Store

Jackson may have an Albertsons, K-Mart, Smith's, Whole Grocer, and Lucky's Market, but only Wilson has Hungry Jack's General Store. At 2,500 square feet, it's not big, but it's got everything from Campbell's soup to clothing. And then there's the canoe hanging from the ceiling.

Clarence "Stearnie" and Dodie Stearns bought the Wilson Market in 1954, when it was across the street from its present location. The couple, who met while working in Yellowstone and married in 1949, changed the name to Hungry Jack's and expanded from a grocery store to a general store. It moved to its present location in 1967 and it's possible an inventory hasn't been taken since.

One of the few general stores left in Wyoming, you can walk into Hungry Jack's for a banana or beer and walk out not only with those items, but also a whole new outfit . . . if you can find your way out. While stores traditionally organize their aisles in a grid, Hungry Jack's aisles are a labyrinth of concentric circles. Within the circles are groceries, 60-pound buckets of Wonderful Wyoming brand honey, western-styled, handmade Cattle Kate silk scarves, Carhartt pants, Woolrich shirts, and Lost Horizons wool hats and gloves.

The hanging canoe—a wooden Old Town model that belonged to Elt Davis, a ranger in Grand Teton National Park in the 1950s—and other memorabilia scattered throughout the store speak to Stearnie and Dodie's lives. (Stearnie died in January 2015 at age 94.) The couple were avid canoeists and the store sold canoes for decades. Stearnie started paddling at age 16, guiding muskie fishermen in his home state of Minnesota for $3 a day. The belt hanging above an old pair of telemark skis on a wall belonged to Stearnie. He was the first paid professional ski patroller at Snow King and only one of two patrol-lers from the northern Rockies to be chosen to be on the 1960 Olympic Ski Patrol at Squaw Valley. The belt on the wall is the one he wore while working the Games. Stearnie and Dodie both have lifetime passes to JHMR.

Stearnie and Dodie sold the store to their daughter and son-in-law, Jana and Kevin Roice, in 1989, and the young couple knew better than to mess with anything.

↓ Nora's Fish Creek Inn

Come to Nora's Fish Creek Inn for Jackson Hole's best breakfast—everything from trout and eggs to banana bread French toast, huevos rancheros, and biscuits and gravy—and linger for the people watching. Long before the James Beard Foundation recognized Nora's in 2012 as one of "America's Classics" and Guy Fieri featured it in 2014 on *Diners, Drive-Ins, and Dives*, locals from construction workers to congressmen and cowboys knew how special this place was and sat elbow to elbow at its U-shaped bar. They still do. Nora's isn't just Jackson Hole's best breakfast, but also one of the valley's most authentically local restaurants. Opened in 1982, today it's run by Nora's kids, Kathryn and Trace. *norasfishcreekinn.com*

NICK COTE

NICK COTE

↑ Stagecoach Band

"You have the privilege tonight of hearing the worst country western band in the US," band manager Bill Briggs used to tell the crowd gathered to dance at the metal-roofed Stagecoach Bar at the base of Teton Pass in Wilson every Sunday night. Bill was being modest though. Thirty-some years ago, *Skiing* magazine actually named the Stagecoach Band "the worst country western band in the *Western Hemisphere*." That was then though. "The Stagecoach Band has been many things over many years—professional players and rank amateurs," says Phil Round, who has been playing with the band since the early 1980s and plays about forty Sundays a year now. "But there have never been as good players in the band as there are now."

Phil says being singled out by *Skiing* was "quite a badge of distinction" at the time though. "Here it's cool to be a climbing bum, or a skiing bum. It gave the band a dirt bag identity and everybody was quite proud of it."

Since its first show February 16, 1969, the Stagecoach Band has never rehearsed. (The band's subtitle has always been "high-risk music.") It has played every single Sunday except for the ones that coincide with Christmas Day. (And it only skips Christmas because the Stagecoach Bar is closed that day.) The band has witnessed—and assisted with—the bar's transformation from rough and seedy to a community treasure. For some time now, locals have been calling Sunday nights at the bar "church." Church is one of the best dance scenes in the valley.

Since it doesn't rehearse, the band doesn't bother with song lists either. "One guy will start a song and the others will fall in," Phil says. "Today that usually works, but we had periods when you'd get to the end of a song and there'd be two guys who didn't know what key it was in."

The Stagecoach Band celebrates its fiftieth anniversary in 2019. *stage coachbar.net*

LOCAL LOWDOWN

PHIL ROUND, Member of the Stagecoach Band

Phil Round has been a professional musician in Jackson Hole since the early 1980s. He was a founding member of the bluegrass band Loose Ties, which won Best New Band at the Telluride Bluegrass Festival and placed second at the 1986 Best New Acoustic Group competition in Louisville, Kentucky. Catch Phil most Sundays with the Stagecoach Band and Thursday through Saturday evenings in the lobby of the Amangani hotel.

NICK COTE

Q: *What brought you to Jackson Hole?*

PHIL ROUND: I took a semester off from college and came out to ski the '77–'78 season.

Q: *Did you ever make it back to college?*

PR: I ended up spending more than the planned semester away, but did eventually go back. I got a degree in geology and was back here permanently in 1980.

Q: *What was your first gig?*

PR: It might have been with the Stagecoach Band. I sat in with them a few times around 1980 and then started playing more regularly with them a year or so later. I came around after most of the bar fighting had stopped, but I was there when cowboys could still ride their horses inside and up to the bar.

Q: *How'd you get the gig at Amangani?*

PR: At some function at a ranch in Hoback Canyon, the general manager asked me if I was interested, and I turned him down. I wasn't interested in a house gig.

Q: *And then?*

PR: Not that I was trying to do this, but

there's nothing like turning someone down to make you more desirable. He eventually convinced me to come and check out the scene. I went up for lunch and brought a guitar and sat in a corner of the lobby and was just blown away by the acoustics. I thought I'd try it for a week or so; now it's been over 13 years. It was totally serendipitous.

Q: *Why is Jackson special to you?*

PR: I think people here humble themselves to this place rather than asking the place to provide them with all of the things they want. The fact that you can go out into the woods today and be killed by a grizzly bear–that's a wonderful thing. That's how nature should be.

↓ Streetfood

When Marcos Hernandez and Amelia Hatchard went on their first date, neither spoke the other's language. They married 6 months later. "It was fast, but we knew it was right," Amelia says. They've now been married for 10 years. When the couple found an opportunity to open a restaurant—they met working at the Westbank Grill at the Four Seasons Resort Jackson Hole—it happened only 7 weeks after their first serious conversation about renting the space. "That was more of an 'Oh My God moment,'" Amelia says. From the start though, locals knew Streetfood was right. Summers at the restaurant are so busy now the 30-something couple has to come up with a way to give the kitchen a break. "We're maybe thinking about a taco truck out front or something," Amelia says.

NICK COTE

NICK COTE

While Amelia has formal training from Le Cordon Bleu in Paris, much of the menu at Streetfood comes from the recipes of Marcos's mom, Carmela. ("We make different salsa though," Marcos says. "Hers is too hot.") Marcos grew up in Leon, Guanajuheo, 4 hours south of Mexico City, and was the youngest of eleven kids. During the day, Carmela managed the cafeteria at a factory with 1,000 workers. She'd come home from this job and cook for her family. "We tried to cook for ourselves," Marcos says, "but she never let us. She was excited to make us dinner."

Carmela hasn't yet visited Jackson or Streetfood, but "she is happy with the idea" people in Wyoming are eating her recipes, Marcos says. But there is one condition. "She told me I have to make everything fresh. 'If you do something frozen I'll be disappointed in you,'" she said. Amelia says, "We would never want to do it any other way. It'd certainly be easier if we didn't make everything ourselves–our chicken tinga requires a full day of prep time–but we'll never change that. We don't think food has to be fancy, but it has to be fresh." *streetfoodjh.com*

STREETFOOD'S MAHI MAHI FISH TACOS

Marcos grew up eating these mahi mahi tacos on Fridays during Lent. The slaw is his addition to his mom's traditional recipe.

MAKES 12 TACOS

NICK COTE

FISH

1½ pounds mahi mahi or similar firm white fish

½ bunch of cilantro, chopped

2 cloves of garlic, diced fine

Olive oil as needed

Salt and pepper as needed

Chop the fish, and then marinate with olive oil, cilantro, and fresh diced garlic. Sauté the fish in a large pan on medium-high heat. Season as needed.

SLAW

1 head of red cabbage, sliced

4 tomatoes, diced

1 red onion, diced

½ bunch cilantro, chopped

Olive oil

Mix fresh cabbage, red onions, tomatoes, cilantro, and olive oil. Season with black pepper and salt.

SALSA VERDE

6 tomatillos

1 jalapeno (more if you want spicy salsa)

1 garlic clove

½ bunch of cilantro, stems removed

Boil tomatillos and jalapenos in water, until the tomatillos and jalapenos feel soft, about 20 minutes. Cool, then puree the tomatillos and jalapenos with just enough cooking liquid to blend smooth. Add garlic and cilantro, and then season to taste.

To plate, heat corn tortillas on both sides until soft. Top tortillas with fish, slaw, and salsa verde. Serve with fresh lime wedges.

◆ ROAD TRIP 3
ART AND CULTURE

Jackson Hole drew artists long before it drew art collectors. It was Thomas Moran's paintings that he created while traveling through the area in 1872 that helped convince Congress to designate that land as the world's first national park. Today the valley is home to some of the country's finest western and wildlife painters and sculptors (both traditional and contemporary), nearly thirty art galleries, and the National Museum of Wildlife Art. The valley has a resident symphony orchestra in the summer too.

GRAND TETON MUSIC FESTIVAL, RUDOLF COSTIN

↓ Art for the Ears

"One of the world's great orchestras is hidden in a small town in Wyoming," Zubin Mehta, the former music director of the New York Philharmonic, once said. The small town he was referring to is Teton Village and the orchestra is the one that plays during the Grand Teton Music Festival (GTMF). For 7 weeks every summer—early July through mid-August—the music festival brings together the country's—and world's—finest orchestral musicians, guest conductors, and soloists. Orchestra concerts are Friday and Saturday; Tuesday, Wednesday, and Thursday are "spotlight" concerts highlighting ensembles and genres of music.

The Grand Teton Music Festival was founded in 1962 and has come a long way since. In its earliest years, performances were held in the old Jackson

GRAND TETON MUSIC FESTIVAL

Hole High School gymnasium, at Jackson Lake Lodge, and on the lawn of St. John's Church. In 1967, the orchestra began performing in Teton Village. Full orchestra concerts were outside, under a carnival tent. Chamber performances were inside the Mangy Moose Saloon. It wasn't until 1974 that Walk Festival Hall, at the base of the Jackson Hole Mountain Resort, opened, and it wasn't until 2007 that the hall had heat installed. (Since then, while the main Grand Teton Music Festival season remains the summer, the group has hosted winter performances.)

While Grand Teton Music Festival has only had three music directors over its fifty-plus years—Ling Tung (1968–1996), Eiji Oue (1997–2003), and Donald Runnicles (2006–present)—dozens of soloists and conductors have performed with the group. The list reads like a who's who of classical music: violinist Itzhak Perlman, pianist Yefin Bronfman, soprano Christine Brewer, conductor Zubin Mehta, and the Mormon Tabernacle Choir, among others. Orchestra members love Grand Teton Music Festival as much as audiences. More than a dozen musicians have been playing in the orchestra for over 25 years. A couple have played for more than 40 years. *gtmf.org*

LOCAL LOWDOWN
JIM WILCOX

Over the course of his almost 50-year career as an artist, Jim Wilcox has won some of the most prestigious awards in the western wildlife genre. When he first moved to Jackson full time, however, not one of the three galleries in town was interested in representing him. So he and wife, Narda, rented a space "about the size of a large bathroom," Wilcox says, and sold his paintings of the Tetons from it. As Wilcox's own artistic career became more successful, so did Wilcox Gallery, which now represents several dozen other artists.

Q: *Did you always want to be a painter?*

JIM WILCOX: I decided halfway through college I'd rather live in Jackson Hole and paint than be in a smoky office in some city.

Q: *So you moved here right after college?*

JW: No. I was willing to be poor if need be to be an artist, but I wasn't willing to starve. I taught art for a couple of years in Seattle after graduation, and we spent summers in Jackson when I'd paint and sell what I could. Finally, I sold enough one summer I thought we could make it.

Q: *But then no galleries would represent you, right?*

JW: None of them was interested in having my work.

Q: *What were you painting at the time?*

JW: The Tetons were the only subject I was interested in painting. I only did foregrounds because I needed somewhere to place the mountains.

Q: *What is it about the Tetons that appeal to you as an artist?*

JW: The Tetons are really complex, especially when they have snow on them. They are some of the most difficult mountains to paint because they are so iconic. When you paint them, you're almost painting a portrait—you have to be that accurate because everyone knows what they look like. Painting them is intimidating, and I was very intimidated painting them early on. I don't paint them because they're easy, but because they're exciting to me.

Q: *What finally inspired you to paint something other than the Tetons?*

JW: I went out to paint the Tetons one day and I looked east and the clouds were so exciting. I painted them instead.

NICK COTE

↑ *Plein Air* Painting

"It's really important as a landscape painter to spend time outside," says Kathryn Mapes Turner, a Jackson Hole painter whose watercolors and oils of landscapes, horses, and wildlife are included in museum collections across the country and at Trio Fine Art in Jackson. "That's where the initial seeds of inspiration come from. You see nuances and subtleties that can't be captured even with photographs."

Turner is one of many local landscape artists who spend time outside painting. A French term for this has been universally adopted: *en plein air*. It translates literally as "in full air." A *plein air* painting is one that was painted outside, usually with its subject matter in full view.

Drive into Grand Teton National Park almost any summer day and you're sure to see at least one painter with her box easel set up alongside the road. "The practice of plein air painting is just really fun," says Turner, who was born as the fourth generation to be raised on the Triangle X Ranch in Grand Teton National Park (GTNP). "There's spending quality time with the landscape and noticing subtle stuff photos don't capture, and also there are challenges around painting outside you don't get in the controlled environment of a studio."

Turner's had her easel blown over more times than she can remember, has been eaten alive by bugs, gotten mildly hypothermic, and, once at Oxbow Bend, had a moose swim across the Snake River and emerge just in front of her. "I had been standing there for so long and was so still that it didn't even notice me. It shook itself dry right in front of my canvas," says Turner.

If you want to increase your chances of finding an artist painting plein air, look for the annual July event "Plein Air for the Park," sponsored in partnership by the Rocky Mountain Plein Air Painters, the Grand Teton Association, and Grand Teton National Park.

The National Museum of Wildlife Art also has a plein air event, "Plein Air Fest Etc.," in mid- to late June. Held on the museum's Sculpture Trail, which looks out on the National Elk Refuge and the Gros Ventre Mountains, you can walk behind the artists and watch each develop their painting over several hours. At the end of the event, the fresh paintings are auctioned off.

Under usual circumstances–i.e., when they're not required to finish a piece for immediate sale–plein air painters have different processes. Jennifer Hoffman, who owns Trio Fine Art in downtown Jackson with fellow valley painters Bill Sawczuk and Kathryn Mapes Turner, uses studies she creates plein air to do larger works in her studio. "Most of the stuff I do in the field is small," she says. She also tends to shy away from the valley's jaw-dropping views. "I do paint the Tetons occasionally, but I am generally drawn to smaller, more intimate things. I never get tired of painting aspens–they're different in every kind of light and in every season." Hoffman also loves painting in the South Park area. "With the Snake River running through and Flat Creek and all the willows–the patterns and textures are interesting to me," she says. Hoffman also likes painting in the snow. One February, she did twenty-eight plein air paintings, one per day for the entire month. Turner says plein air painting is "as addictive as fly fishing or skiing. It's an *experience*; you're doing so much more than just painting."

Jackson Hole's First Art Gallery

Today you can't throw a snowball in downtown Jackson without hitting an art gallery. But in 1963 when Dick Flood Sr. decided to open a gallery here, he hid what he was doing for as long as possible. Because there wasn't a single art gallery in the valley, he had an inkling, which proved to be correct, that locals would think his idea was crazy, but he didn't want to be talked out of it. Flood instructed the man painting the name he had chosen–"Trailside Galleries"– on the gallery to do it *Wheel of Fortune*–style (in other words, not to paint the

LOCAL LOWDOWN
MARIAM DIEHL, Owner of Diehl Gallery

A Manhattan transplant, Irish-Iraqi Mariam Diehl bought Meyer Gallery in 2005 after working there for 3 years. At the time, the gallery represented only traditional western and wildlife artists. Since then, this equestrienne—Mariam had been a volunteer mounted officer with the New York City Parks Enforcement Patrol—has not only renamed the gallery but also transformed it. Today it is one of the valley's most contemporary galleries, representing artists including Donald Martiny and Hung Liu and traveling to national exhibitions like Chicago's SOFA.

While many people who end up spending time in Jackson Hole do not plan on landing here permanently, Mariam did. "I was ready to leave New York and researched small mountain towns in the West," she says. "When I stumbled upon Jackson, I knew right away I'd found my future home. And when I landed a job and moved here, it was everything I knew it would be—spectacularly beautiful with a tremendous number of outdoor pursuits available within spitting distance of the front door and

NICK COTE

full of interesting people. And you can see the New York City Ballet—I love that."

When Mariam says there are outdoor pursuits spitting distance from the door, she's not exaggerating. The home she shares with husband Scott and son Quinlan is on the Snake River. They can cast a line into the river from their backyard. She has to drive to horseback ride however. "My current favorite riding spot is in the Snake River Canyon down in the river bottom below Astoria Hot Springs," she says, "though Emma Matilda Lake always takes my breath away. And I love riding to Phelps Lake and swimming with the horses."

JACKSON'S ART SCENE

"When I started in the gallery world here, there was a very small contemporary art scene and since then it has blossomed," Mariam Diehl says. "It's still not huge, but it exists, which is pretty fantastic for a small mountain town." Top galleries to check out include Diehl Gallery, Tayloe Piggott Gallery, Altamira Gallery, and Heather James Fine Art.

According to Mariam, there are three artsy things visitors to the valley should do:

1. Walk the Sculpture Trail at the National Museum of Wildlife Art at dawn or dusk.
2. Check out the current installation in the outdoor courtyard at the Center for the Arts.
3. See the exhibition in the Art Association Gallery.

letters in order). Eventually the lettering was completed, and Flood couldn't hide his gallery any longer.

Because Flood was a passionate collector of western and wildlife art, that's what Trailside Galleries specialized in. It had works by Charles Russell, Olaf Wieghorst, Ernie Berke, Nick Eggenhofer, Ned Jacob, and Asa Powell. Trailside Galleries has moved around the Town Square several times since it opened and has changed ownership, but it still specializes in western and wildlife art.

↓ National Museum of Wildlife Art

You'd be hard-pressed to guess that what started the National Museum of Wildlife Art (NMWA)–celebrating its thirtieth anniversary in 2017–was a small painting titled "Favorite Panfish" bought from a gallery in Minnesota. In 1962, Joffa Kerr gave this painting by artist Les C. Kouba to her husband, Bill, to celebrate his graduation from law school. The next summer, they bought another painting, "Trophy Mule Deer," by Frank Hoffman. The year after that, the couple bought their first "big" painting, Carl Rungius's "Wanderers Above Timberline." It was such a big purchase they had to make it on layaway.

NIKITA MAMOCHINE

↓ THE NMWA'S SCULPTURE TRAIL

National Museum of Wildlife Art Petersen Curator of Art and Research Adam Harris says a sculpture trail was something the museum had been thinking and talking about even before he started working there. Harris started at the museum in 2000. The sculpture trail opened in 2012. Now that it's happened, no one denies it was worth the wait, mostly because, by waiting so long, the timing worked out for California-based landscape architect Walter Hood to design it. Prior to the National Museum of Wildlife Art Sculpture Trail, Hood's best-known projects included gardens at San Francisco's De Young Museum, community parks in Oakland, and two public spaces in Pittsburgh's Hill District. The National Museum of Wildlife Art project was Hood's first in Wyoming. "I've probably never worked in such a changing landscape," says Hood. "Every visit, I saw something else."

And what Hood was seeing wasn't what the National Museum of Wildlife Art saw. "They wanted a trail around a parking lot," he says. "I said that that'd be awful." What the museum ended up with is a gently undulating trail that winds ¾ of a mile along the edge of a butte overlooking the National Elk Refuge. Along the trail, there are Douglas fir benches and, of course, sculptures. Pieces here are made of bronze, wood, and metal, and depict wildlife of all kinds, from a horned toad to an isis (this sculpture is 10 feet tall) and a herd of seven bison. The bison piece, by artist Richard Loffler, is the largest sculpture in the museum's collection—it's 64 feet long. The trail is free and, in the summer, home to live music, theater, and even yoga.

NIKITA MAMOCHINE

Fast forward 25 years to 1987. The Kerrs had one of the finest collections of wildlife and sporting art in the country. At that time, there weren't any museums dedicated to or even exhibiting the genre on any real scale. (Some in the art world didn't even consider it fine art.) So the Kerrs, along with a handful of other Jackson Hole locals, started their own museum, renting 5,000 square feet of space on Jackson's Town Square and naming it Wildlife of the American West. Their collection formed the backbone of the new museum's holdings, but was regularly supplemented with visiting exhibits from other sources. And then the Kerrs kept collecting. By 1993, Wildlife of the American West had outgrown its space and went looking for a new home, and a new name.

In September 1994, the National Museum of Wildlife Art, then constructed out of 4,033 tons of Arizona sandstone (which was replaced in 2011 by Idaho quartzite), opened on WY 89 just north of downtown. The heart of the collection remained the pieces from Joffa and Bill Kerr, but, in total, the museum had over 1,000 wildlife and sporting works of art. At the opening ceremonies, Bill Kerr said, "May [this museum] long serve those who come to this place in search of the wild, the natural, the forgotten, and the serene."

When the museum turned fifteen, Bob Koenke, the publisher of *Wildlife Art* magazine said of it, "The National Museum of Wildlife Art is to animal art what Cooperstown is to baseball." In April 2008, then-President George W. Bush signed a bill that named the NMWA as *the* National Museum of Wildlife Art of the United States. And it all started with a fish.

By the museum's thirtieth anniversary, the permanent collection included nearly 5,000 pieces that included the work of John J. Audubon, Carl Rungius, Charles Russell, John Clymer, and Albert Bierstadt, as well as Georgia O'Keeffe, Andy Warhol, and Pablo Picasso. Works range from paintings to 4,500-year-old stone carvings and even a 24-foot-tall totem pole.

While the National Museum of Wildlife Art definitely complements Jackson Hole's art scene, its location here makes sense on an even greater scale. "Jackson Hole is in the middle of the Greater Yellowstone Ecosystem," National Museum of Wildlife Art Petersen Curator of Art and Research Adam Harris says. "We're at the bottom of this amazing corridor that goes from Yellowstone up to the Yukon for large animal migrations. There is this whole synchronicity happening between what is happening outside our building, the architecture of our building, and then what you can see inside." *wildlifeart.org*

SEÑOR LOPEZ

Most of the subjects in wildlife art are unknown. "We don't often know who that moose in a painting is," says National Museum of Wildlife Art curator Adam Harris. But we do know the jaguar in two of Anna Vaugh Hyatt Huntington's sculptures in the National Museum of Wildlife Art's permanent collection. He is "Señor Lopez." Señor Lopez was brought to the New York Zoological Society (now the Bronx Zoo) in 1902. "Knowing who an animal was can add a whole other level of interest and interpretation," Harris says. For instance, we know that, while sailing to the United States, Señor Lopez had a mouth infection of some sort. His handlers treated this by rubbing cocaine on the sore area.

Arriving safely in New York, Señor Lopez was installed in an area of the zoo that had access to a room with large panes of glass purpose-built to allow artists to study the animals on the other side. Huntington spent hours observing Señor Lopez before sculpting him.

Jackson Hole Fall Arts Festival

Well into the 1980s, it was a bush that heralded the beginning and end of the season for Jackson Hole's art galleries. You can still see it today. Stand on the southeast corner of Jackson's Town Square and look up to the northwest until your eyes hit the only bush on a hillside of grass and sage. That's it. When this bush's leaves began changing color (into a brilliant red) and falling off, usually around Labor Day, the galleries in town knew summer crowds would soon follow. So they closed their doors until the leaves—and visitors—came back around Memorial Day.

There weren't nearly as many art galleries in Jackson in the early 1980s as there are now, but the handful that existed outnumbered all other retail establishments combined. So when the Jackson Hole Chamber of Commerce made it their mission to extend the town's tourist season beyond June, July, and August, it was reasonable that they looked at what they might do with art. The first Jackson Hole Fall Arts Festival was held in September 1985.

In the ensuing years, the fall arts festival, always held in mid-September, has become one of the busiest times of year in the valley, and it is one of the largest, most diverse festivals of its kind in the country. For 2 weeks, there are concerts, special gallery shows, a fashion show, auctions, street fairs, food events, a design conference, ranch tours, and artists-in-residence. *jacksonholechamber.com*

◆ ROAD TRIP 4
DOWNTOWN JACKSON

Jackson is the largest town—it's the only official town actually—in the valley of Jackson Hole. Jackson is different things to different visitors. It's a throwback to the Wild West, a center for western and wildlife art, or a place to get good food. Chances are that whatever you're looking for (unless it's a Prada or Gucci store—Jackson is really trying not to become another Aspen), Jackson has it.

NICK COTE

↑ Elk Antler Arches

It's a toss-up whether the Tetons or the elk antler arches at the four corners of Jackson's Town Square are more photographed by visitors. When the local Rotary Club erected the first arch in 1953, it had no idea it was creating an icon. But the arch was an instant hit with visitors, so the club started planning for additional arches, one on each corner. These were built between 1966 and 1969. (The southwest corner was the first to get its arch.)

Today's arches are not the original ones though. Elk antlers have a lifespan. "They were starting to decompose," says Rotarian Pete Karns. "People could and did steal individual antlers because they weren't secure anymore." Karns, whose grandfather homesteaded in Jackson in 1890, also realized the arches were becoming a safety hazard. Kids, and adults, climb on them. But "a Jackson Hole without its arches could never exist," he says. In 2006, Karns turned to the valley's three Rotary clubs to fund raise money to replace all four arches. Even the youngest arch looked pretty dingy. "They don't look very good when they're old," Karns says. Ideally, the antlers should be replaced every 30 to 40 years.

The oldest arch, the southwest one, was rebuilt first in 2007. Because this arch is the most popular one for photographs, it wasn't just replaced, but also moved. It was only a matter of time before someone walking backward to take a photo stepped into traffic and was hurt. The southeast arch was redone in 2009, the northeast corner in 2011, and the northwest one in 2013. Each time, workers disassembled the old arch just after Memorial Day and had the new one up by the Fourth of July.

Making an elk antler arch is a labor-intensive process. Workers weave ant-lers—each of which weighs from 5 to 10 pounds—together around the steel frame. Antlers go up one at a time. By the time an arch is done, it's a mosaic of 10,000 to 12,000 pounds of antlers. Some of them are screwed down to add extra support and prevent vandalism. About 1,000 to 2,000 pounds of the antlers in each arch came from the Jackson Hole Boy Scouts, who pick them up on the National Elk Refuge each year. The rest were bought from antler dealers in the Mountain West. The new arches should be good until 2040 or so.

WOODEN SIDEWALKS

The wooden sidewalks around Jackson might be just for show today, but that wasn't always the case. Like most western towns in the early 1900s, Jackson was often mired in mud or worse (remember, horses were the main mode of transportation then). In 1920, Jackson elected the country's first all-female municipal government. These women quickly found funds to build the town's first sidewalks out of wood rather than concrete.

LOCAL LOWDOWN
MARK "FISH" FISHMAN, DJ for KMTN/Jackson Hole

In 1989, Mark "Fish" Fishman moved to Jackson Hole for a summer. The plan was to then return home to Atlanta, marry his college girlfriend, and then go into the restaurant world or maybe work for CNN. "But I wasn't going to be an on-air guy," he says. Fish is still here, and he is definitely an "on-air guy." His voice has been a constant at KMTN (96.9 FM) almost since he arrived. He started at the station—he did the overnight shift the same day he was hired, which was also the same day he interviewed for the job—several months after moving here. Then he did afternoons for several years while working in different restaurants. (At one point, he was assistant food and beverage manager at Spring Creek Ranch.) In 1996, Fish became the station's program director and switched to doing the weekday morning show, which includes the iconic Trash & Treasure segment, where listeners can call and sell (or give away) almost anything.

Q: How do you describe Trash & Treasure?

MARK FISHMAN: It's the original Craigslist.

Q: Have you ever bought anything on Trash & Treasure?

MF: My first summer here I bought a bike.

Q: You've hosted T&T forever. How many other hosts have there been?

MF: More people have walked on the moon than hosted Trash & Treasure. There have only been three of us. Before me there was Brad Brown and Russ Graham.

Q: When did you become "Fish"?

MF: The earliest I remember being called Fish by everyone was third grade. And then in 1979, my mom remarried, to a guy named Mark. So from that point, the family always called me Fish. I'm Uncle Fish. My mom calls me Fish.

Q: Is there a "Fish" personality?

MF: I'm always just being me and I often get the comment from people when they meet me, "Oh, you're just like you are on the radio." I don't try to be "the radio guy." I think listeners like being talked to, not talked at.

Q: Would you ever give up being on the air?

MF: No. It is my tie to the community. Some people fish, or bike, or hike, or ski every day. That is their Jackson Hole thing. As much as I love those things, the ties I've developed to the community through being on the air—that's my Jackson Hole thing.

NICK COTE

WORT HOTEL

Jackson's only National Historic Hotel of America, the Wort opened in 1941 when downtown's streets were still dirt and cowboys were king. The dirt is long gone, but little else has changed on this hotel's exterior, including the red rock trim the Wort brothers quarried themselves in the Gros Ventre Mountains bordering the east side of the valley. Inside the hotel's Silver Dollar Bar, hundreds of uncirculated silver dollar coins are inlaid into the wooden bar top. *worthotel.com*

LOCAL LOWDOWN
ALI AND KEVIN COHANE, Founders and Owners
of Picnic and Persephone Bakery Café

Kevin Cohane took his first kitchen job in the valley—at Blue Lion in 2003—so he could spend his days skiing. Having studied biology and taken a fair amount of chemistry in college, the Connecticut native quickly became attracted to the precision and science of baking. Baking didn't give him the rush skiing did, but he liked the challenge.

In 2007, he put skiing on hold to move to Paris to spend a year studying pastry at Le Cordon Bleu culinary school. Back stateside, he spent 2 years practicing what he had learned at Fox & Obel bakery in Chicago's Streeterville. Eventually he and then-fiancée Ali "really wanted to get something of our own going," he says. They found a 1,700-square-foot location where they could make breads and pastries for wholesale. Persephone Bakery was born.

Ali, who is trained in graphic design, always wanted a retail space. It took the 30-somethings a couple of years, but they eventually found the perfect spot, which Ali describes as a "tiny, cozy cabin that, because it's a bit beaten up, has tons of character." The location isn't bad either: It's one block east of the Town Square.

While Kevin concentrated on making the best croissants outside of Paris, Ali worked hard to establish a "cute, French vintage bakery" vibe inside Persephone Bakery Café.

Walking into the cabin, the first thing you'll notice—after the marble counter overflowing with baked goods—is the wall covered with wooden spoons. "We built Persephone on a budget, and I was trying to come up with something that could fill a big wall but not be super expensive," she says. "Initially we were going to do it with vintage rolling pins, and I soon realized they would be a nightmare to hang. I found a wholesaler of wooden spoons and was excited that since they were all the same I could create a cool graphic. I had to tape them all to the wall three separate times before I got it right." *persephonebakery.com*

PERSEPHONE'S OATMEAL, CRANBERRY, TOFFEE COOKIES
MAKES 16 COOKIES

INGREDIENTS

12.3 ounces unsalted butter

13.4 ounces brown sugar

2 large eggs

¾ teaspoon vanilla extract

10.2 ounces all-purpose flour

1 teaspoon baking soda

1 teaspoon iodized salt

½ teaspoon ground cinnamon

13 ounces regular oats

12.5 ounces Craisins

5 ounces toffee pieces

INSTRUCTIONS

Cream butter and sugar until combined.

Stream in egg and vanilla.

Add flour, baking soda, salt, and cinnamon. Mix until dough just comes together.

Add oats, Craisins, and toffee. Mix until evenly dispersed.

Bake in a convection oven at 350 degrees for 18 minutes.

NICK COTE

◆ ROAD TRIP 5
PUBLIC LANDS

Almost as soon as you exit Yellowstone to the south, you're in Grand Teton National Park. The Tetons, the heart of the park, dominate Jackson Hole, but these mountains and the national park that protects them are only a small fraction of Jackson Hole's public lands. Jackson Hole has the Bridger-Teton National Forest, the National Elk Refuge, and the Gros Ventre and Jedediah Smith Wilderness Areas. All told, 97 percent of the land in Jackson Hole is protected in some way.

Teton Crest Trail

It's arguable there are more scenic backpacking adventures to be had in Jackson Hole than the Teton Crest Trail, but this would be a difficult argument to win. The Crest Trail runs upwards of 40 miles close to the crest of the range. In its entirety, it ascends four passes, traverses the Death Canyon Shelf, crosses Alaska Basin, and skirts Marion, Sunset, and Holly Lakes and Lake Solitude. The trail's average elevation is 10,000 feet.

Fritiof Fryxell, a geologist, climber, and Grand Teton National Park's first naturalist from 1929 to 1934, was the first person to envision a single trail running the length of the range. His earliest notes about it, in 1929, to park superintendent Samuel Woodring, described it as "a summit route tying together all of the proposed canyon feeder trails." That summer, Woodring, as excited at the prospect of this trail as Fryxell, led a small group on horseback into the range to scout potential routes. The idea was to create a trail that took significant time for people to explore. Less than a decade later, thanks in large part to work by the Civilian Conservation Corps, the Crest Trail was born. (At the time though, it was called the Skyline Trail.)

Because of the geology of the Tetons, with canyons every 4 to 6 miles extending into the range like arthritic fingers, you don't have to do the trail's full 45 miles from Phillips Pass to String Lake. Pick your canyon—Granite, Open, Death—head west, and you will connect with the Crest Trail. The most popular route is to take the tram up to the 10,450-foot summit of Rendezvous

Bridger-Teton National Forest is 125 percent the size of Yellowstone.
GLORIA WADZINSKI – ISTOCK

Peak at Jackson Hole Mountain Resort in the Bridger-Teton National Forest and hike west to Marion Lake in Grand Teton National Park and then come out to Jenny Lake, at the mouth of Cascade Canyon. This is usually done over 3 days.

Bridger-Teton National Forest

Grand Teton National Park is the wild land Jackson Hole is most famous for, but "the values that people like about the park wouldn't exist without all of the other lands around here," says Linda Merigliano. "You can't just have national parks in isolation, especially not with the wildlife and conservation we have here."

The 3.4-million-acre BTNF (that's almost eleven times bigger than GTNP and about 125 percent the size of Yellowstone) includes three wilderness areas, more than 2,000 miles of hiking trails, and thirty-seven developed campgrounds, and is home to at least 355 species of birds. It is a significant chunk of the Greater Yellowstone Ecosystem, the 34,375-square-mile zone including and around Yellowstone that is one of the largest nearly intact temperate-zone ecosystems on the planet. This means that today's GYE has the same significant plant and animal species as it did before the arrival of European colonists.

The BTNF is adjacent to Yellowstone and Grand Teton National Parks and the National Elk Refuge. It fringes the town of Jackson to the east and south. Starting from the Town Square, walk 10 minutes in either of these directions and you'll be in the BTNF. Linda says she agrees with a friend of hers who says, "People come for the Tetons, but stay for the national forest." *www.fs .usda.gov/btnf*

↓ National Elk Refuge

When it was founded in 1912, the National Elk Refuge wasn't the country's first wildlife refuge–that honor goes to Pelican Island, off the coast of Florida, which President Teddy Roosevelt established by executive order in 1903–but it was the first wildlife sanctuary specifically created for a terrestrial mammal and referred to as a "refuge."

About 6,000 to 7,000 elk migrate onto the refuge each winter. As impressive as this is, as recently as 130 years ago, tens of thousands of elk passed through Jackson Hole in autumn and then again in late spring. It is estimated that elk in North America once numbered 10 million, inhabiting most areas of the country. By the early 1900s, however, numbers had dropped to 50,000, plummeting just as bison numbers did. Elk were hunted for their hides, meat,

LOCAL LOWDOWN
LINDA MERIGLIANO, Program Manager for Bridger-Teton National Forest

Linda Merigliano was majoring in marine biology when she got a job as a seasonal ranger in the northern Tetons. She had been to the Tetons as a kid with her family and, when she saw this job posting, thought, "Yeah, I'd love to go back there." Linda so loved working in the Tetons and in the backcountry that as soon as she returned to college—it was her senior year—she changed her major to natural resource management. "I spent the whole year taking natural resources–related courses I should have taken earlier," she says. Merigliano made up all the coursework for her new major, and when she graduated, she got a seasonal position with the Forest Service in the Palisades area, near Swan Valley, Idaho.

Linda continued working summer seasonal jobs and, in winter, taught skiing at Grand Targhee. When the Jedediah Smith Wilderness became a designated wilderness in 1984, Linda was there rangering. "Alaska Basin [arguably the heart of the Jed Smith and just west of the boundary of GTNP] is home to me," Linda says. "I know that place really, really well and have been up there in all kinds of weather."

After earning a master's degree in wilderness management, Linda traveled the country working as part of a Forest Service team that taught how to put together wilderness implementation schedules. She always returned home to the Tetons. And then, in 1991, the Bridger-Teton National Forest (BTNF) founded a permanent position that was a perfect fit for her as the recreation, wilderness, and trails program manager for the Jackson District of the BTNF. She's been a permanent employee of the BTNF since then and, in 2016, was recognized with the Aldo Leopold Award for Overall Wilderness Stewardship by the US Forest Service.

"I made a very conscious choice to stay here," Linda says. "Jackson is such a unique community—we're a resort, but have every kind of recreation going on here, and also have this conservation history and wildlife resources that don't exist in any other resort community. The people who live here know and value that. My passion is recreation and wild places and the responsible use and care of those places. I want to be in a community where people care about those kinds of things."

With all of the valley's megafauna, it is the pica, a small mammal with big ears and short limbs, that is Linda's favorite animal. "They're such curious critters," she says. "The more you learn about their life cycles, the more fascinating they are. They live in the mountains and live on grass; it's a particularly unique habitat and I think this area is a bit of a stronghold for them." Linda's license plate even reads "PICA."

NICK COTE

The National Elk Refuge is home to nearly 7,000 elk each winter.
NICK COTE

and "ivory" teeth. Despite all this, the Jackson Hole elk herd was somewhat protected, at least until the town of Jackson came along.

Historically, the southern end of Jackson Hole was prime winter range for elk. But with the growth of the town of Jackson, 75 percent of this migration corridor was difficult for elk to get to. They had to navigate homesteads and fences. With only 25 percent of their former winter range available, Jackson Hole elk began to die in mass numbers. Locals saw this and were alarmed. It was too late to move the town at that point, but not too late to begin preserving the land north and east of town. In the summer, there's not much to see on the National Elk Refuge. Elk usually begin migrating from higher ground to the refuge in October and remain until April. In winter, it is possible to take a sleigh ride into the middle of the elk herd. *www.fws.gov/refuge/ national_elk_refuge/*

↓ Sleigh Rides

Sleighs pulled by 2,000-pound Belgian and Percheron draft horses can get much closer to the thousands of elk wintering on the National Elk Refuge than is possible for anyone to do by foot. Wrapped in a blanket on a sleigh, you're literally surrounded by elk. The secret? These elk are accustomed to the sleighs, which have been visiting the herd for more than 100 years. Before there were official sleigh ride tours, there were the feed sleighs, which started running the first winter of the refuge. Generations of elk have grown up around sleighs and know they're not a threat.

US FISH & WILDLIFE SERVICE

↓JENNY LAKE LODGE

Jenny Lake Lodge is often booked out a year in advance, but don't expect over-the-top amenities. This collection of historic log cabins—many date from the 1920s—near the northern end of Jenny Lake doesn't have televisions, and there's only a phone in your room if you request it. Quilts are handmade though, and the lodge's breakfast and five-course dinner (both available to non-guests, with a prior reservation) are among the best meals in the valley.

CODY DOWNARD PHOTOGRAPHY

LOCAL LOWDOWN
MATT HAZARD, Grand Teton National Park
Landscape Architect

COURTESY OF GRAND TETON NATIONAL PARK

When he's not working, the landscape architect heading up the 5-year project to revamp Jenny Lake, including re-doing upwards of 5 miles of trails and all signage, prefers hiking without trails. "I like not knowing where I am," says GTNP landscape architect Matt Hazard, picured on the right in the photo. "I think that slight kind of fear you get from not knowing exactly where you are makes for an adventuresome trip. But that kind of feeling is only good when it's what you want." Hazard says that one of the main reasons the park spent so much time and money on Jenny Lake is that many visitors to the area, the most visited in the park, were feeling lost when they didn't want to be.

A Mississippi native, Matt first hiked around Jenny Lake when he was a kid vacationing in GTNP with his family. "Growing up, I had this appreciation for being out west," he says. Hazard family vacations were often to the West's national parks. Matt remembers hiking down to Phantom Ranch at the bottom of the Grand Canyon when he was eleven. The first time he hiked around Jenny Lake with the eyes of a landscape architect he thought, "Wow, this area needs a lot of work." Matt got confused as to where to start hiking and at several points as he hiked around the lake. "It was a disaster," he says. "One spot in particular was really bad. Park staff called it 'confusion junction.'"

While nearly 2 million people come to Jenny Lake on their vacation, Matt tries to get away from it when he's off work. He likes hiking in Moose Basin, across Jackson Lake, and in Upper and Lower Berry Canyons. "Some of the geological formations up there are unreal," he says. "And there are no people."

In the refuge's early years, people wanting a closer look at the elk could go out on the feed sleighs. By the 1960s though, there were so many people who wanted to ride along there wasn't room, so separate touring sleighs began running. Nowadays they run from 10 a.m. to 4 p.m. every day except Christmas from mid-December through early April, whether it's 30 degrees below zero or 30 degrees above zero. (Every sleigh, which is hand-built, comes with a pile of wool blankets.)

Don't concentrate too much on the elk or you'll miss the other animals that live on the refuge. The refuge is home to more than 150 species of amphibians and birds including bald eagles, sage grouse, and trumpeter swans and forty-five different species of mammals, including moose, bison, bighorn sheep, and pronghorn. *www.fws.gov/refuge/national_elk_refuge/*

Cache Creek

The Cache Creek area, less than 2 miles east of Jackson's Town Square, is the most used area of the Bridger-Teton National Forest (BTNF). Some locals hike or bike here every day. When the BTNF conducts visitor use monitoring surveys, one of the questions asked is, "How many times have you visited the national forest in the last year?" Regarding the Cache Creek trailheads, answers are often, "I might have missed 5 days last year." "When you look at [the BTNF] compared to other forests in the nation, we have one of the highest frequencies of use of any of them," says program manager Linda Merigliano. And Cache Creek is a favorite local spot for a daily connection to nature. Still, there are enough trails—Putt Putt, Hagen, Sidewalk Trail, Serengeti—so that it doesn't feel crowded. The main trail, an abandoned Forest Service road, is the busiest in the drainage, but make it past the first 1.5 miles (the road goes for about 5 miles) and the crowds dwindle to nothing.

Cache Creek isn't just about convenience. It is gorgeous, with trails winding along Cache Creek, moose sightings, and some of the valley's best late-spring wildflowers.

↓ DRY STONE CONSERVANCY

Most of the trails around Jenny Lake, the single busiest spot in Grand Teton National Park and at the mouth of Cascade Canyon, were built by the Civilian Conservation Corps (CCC) back in the 1930s. The CCC crews used mostly dry stone masonry to build trails. An ancient method of building (Egypt's pyramids and Central America's Maya temples used it), dry stone structures can actually become sturdier with wear and time. Still, when the CCC built the Jenny Lake infrastructure in the 1930s, there were only thousands of people who visited the lake. At the turn of the millennium, Jenny Lake was getting millions of visitors every year. The original dry stone masonry needed repair. Unfortunately, it was a dying art.

Dry Stone Conservancy, a Kentucky-based group that trains stonemasons to relearn the craft, came to the rescue. The work Jenny Lake needed was so substantial that the group didn't just train GTNP's trail crew, but sent out a crew of its own to help, and to provide more extensive training than available in a weekend workshop (if you're interested, these are offered in Lexington, Kentucky). Dry Stone Conservancy masons had been trained by a Scottish master stonemason. After years of working alongside the Dry Stone Conservancy pros, GTNP now has its own in-house crew of dry stonemasons.

Walking around Jenny Lake, it's difficult to tear your eyes from the mountains, but, if you do, notice the craftsmanship of the new stone steps on the trail and the new retaining walls . . . not that you'll be able to tell they're new. "One of the cool things about dry stone work is that you can't tell when it was built. It could have been 1900," says Matt Hazard. *gtnpf .org/initiatives/the-campaign-for-jenny-lake*

NIKITA MAMOCHINE

LOCAL LOWDOWN
Grand Teton National Park's Wildlife Brigade

"Bear management is people management," says GTNP bear management specialist Kate Wilmot. With grizzly bears recovering well under the Endangered Species Act, their habitat has expanded south. There's now no doubt these animals are in Grand Teton National Park. (Black bears have always lived in GTNP.) Into the 1990s, there were perhaps a couple of grizzlies living in the park, but only in the most northern areas, in canyons where there are no official hiking trails. At the time, they were so few and so rarely seen, most locals believed they just weren't there. That thinking ended in the early 2000s. The summer of 2004, a grizzly sow and her cub spent much of their time near

NIKITA MAMOCHINE

roads in the northern part of the park. A couple of years later, a sow had a litter of three cubs, and this family also spent much of their time near roads, near Jackson Lake Junction. Word quickly got out that Grand Teton National Park was a great place to see grizzlies.

Since park rangers were already overextended, GTNP came up with a pilot program to manage human and bear interactions, also known as "bear jams." Rather than manage the bears or manage the scene, GTNP's new Wildlife Brigade had the goal of managing the people. "We decided to model ourselves on Yellowstone in this aspect," says Wilmot. "We knew other places that essentially had tried to haze bears away from developed areas and saw that that wasn't working. The way Yellowstone was doing it was successful, so that's what we copied."

GTNP's Wildlife Brigade, which consists mostly of seasonal volunteers (they get an RV spot in exchange for being on the brigade), has been so successful, "we're almost too successful," Wilmot says. "We get called to hornet jams now." She's not kidding. "Park visitors go crazy for almost anything," she says. "And that's great—to see people so excited about seeing wildlife but sometimes that excitement can lead to people making bad decisions, or just doing things that they don't know they shouldn't do."

Wilmot says bear jams are "absolutely insane." Moose are the second most popular. If there is a young moose, you can forget common sense. Big bull moose are also quite

attractive for visitors. Everything else—great grey owls, elk—are still exciting, but don't have the level of insanity. One recent summer, two grizzly sows, both with multiple cubs, hung out in Willow Flats, near Jackson Lake Junction. Often there would be cars parked on the side of the road for more than a mile.

Park rules prohibit "willfully approaching, remaining, viewing, or engaging in any activity within 100 yards of bears or wolves, or within 25 yards of any other wildlife including nesting birds; or within any distance that disturbs, displaces, or otherwise interferes with the free unimpeded movement of wildlife, or creates or contributes to a potentially hazardous condition or situation."

Wildlife Brigade teams—there's a southern one and a northern one—are out daily during the summer season. When there's no wildlife jam to be managed, they patrol campgrounds and parking lots. "Food storage is one of the best things we can do to help bears and people co-exist," Wilmot says. "Of course, we want visitors to see wildlife, but it's our job to protect the wildlife too. And we don't want these bears to think we're nice or have food for them."

NIKITA MAMOCHINE

↑ Laurence Rockefeller Preserve in Grand Teton National Park

At the 1,106-acre Laurence Rockefeller Preserve, a private retreat of the Rockefeller family until it was assumed into GTNP in 2007, parking is limited to fifty cars. Enforcement is by friendly-but-firm preserve staff. People come here for some of the flattest hiking trails in the park, including a 7-mile loop around Phelps Lake, one of the glacial lakes at the base of the Tetons, and also to hang out in high-backed Adirondack chairs in the shade on the interpretive center's front porch. Inside the interpretive center, you'll find a small library, big leather chairs, and a Terry Tempest Williams poem written on a wall. *nps.gov/grte*

Leaving Yellowstone via the East Entrance takes you immediately into Buffalo Bill territory. Two miles outside the park, you'll discover Pahaska Tepee Resort, which Buffalo Bill founded as a hunting lodge. It opened to guests in 1905 and was added to the National Register of Historic Places in 1973. The resort still hosts overnight guests, whether they're hunters or hikers.

The Buffalo Bill connection grows deeper as you head farther away from the park. Travel roughly 50 miles alongside the South Fork of the Shoshone River, and you will arrive in Cody, Wyoming, the town founded by the famous showman. Cody, population 9,800, has matured since the days Buffalo Bill held tryouts for his Wild West show in empty lots around the Irma Hotel, which he named for his daughter. The Buffalo Bill Center of the West is often called the "Smithsonian of the West" and art galleries dot Sheridan Avenue. Still, there's a nightly rodeo, a staged gunfight in downtown, and a family-owned shoe store where staff take pride in custom-making the cowboy boots of your dreams.

GLORIA WADZINSKI

But don't limit yourself to Cody. A visit to the towns of Meeteetse and Thermopolis is a step back in time. In Meeteetse, you can find some of the best homemade chocolate truffles you've ever tasted. Visit Thermopolis and take a soak in mineral hot springs at Wyoming's most popular state park. Then watch paleontologists at the Wyoming Dinosaur Center work on dinosaur fossils excavated nearby.

Yellowstone's East Entrance combines true Wild West history with authentic, small-town charm. There are also wild horses, Wyoming's own "Grand Canyon" (the Bighorn Canyon National Recreation Area), and the Heart Mountain Interpretive Center. Opened in 2011, the center exists to explain what life was like at the Heart Mountain Internment Camp, home to more than 10,000 Japanese Americans from August 1942 to November 1945.

COURTESY HEART MOUNTAIN WYOMING FOUNDATION

◆ ROAD TRIP 1
ALL ROADS LEAD TO CODY

Like the South Entrance, Yellowstone's East Entrance is far removed from civilization. Wapiti is about 20 miles from the East Entrance but has minimal services; Cody is 52 miles away. You might be tempted to rush headlong toward Cody's shops, museums, galleries, and restaurants, but sit back and enjoy the scenery on a meandering drive down the stretch of highway between the East Entrance and Cody. President Teddy Roosevelt once called this "the 50 most beautiful miles in America." He wasn't lying.

Scenic Byways

Twenty-eight miles of US 14/16/20 between the East Entrance and Cody were designated as the Buffalo Bill Cody Scenic Byway in 1991. Wyoming was a

↓ FOREST SERVICE CABIN

The Wapiti Ranger Station, 19 miles east of Pahaska Tepee on US 14, wasn't the first ranger station to be built in the country, but it is now the oldest ranger station still standing. It *was* the first ranger station to be built using federal money. (When early forest rangers Nathaniel Wilkerson and Henry C. Tuttle built the Alta Ranger Station in the Bitterroot National Forest in 1899, which was the first ranger station in the country, they paid for it out of their own pockets and were never reimbursed.) The Wapiti Ranger Station, which was actually two buildings—a log cabin living quarters and a detached office—was built in 1904 from timber collected nearby. In the 100+ years since it was constructed, the structures have been modified—they were joined into a single building—and old logs have been replaced, but it's still in use. *(307) 527-6241*

PARK COUNTY TRAVEL COUNCIL

little slower to recognize the road's uniqueness: It was designated a Wyoming Scenic Byway in 1995.

Leaving Yellowstone, the byway follows the burbling Shoshone River; at many points, the river and road are no more than a cast apart. If you have a Wyoming fishing license, you can cast in the Shoshone. It's considered some of the best fly fishing in the state with brown, rainbow, cutbow, and Yellowstone cutthroat trout.

Elsewhere it might be difficult to tear your gaze from a river as aggressively beautiful as the Shoshone, but here you have locals—bison, grizzly bears, bighorn sheep, elk—vying for your attention. Once you leave the East Entrance, you're still in protected land, the 2.5-million-acre Shoshone National Forest. It is believed that the eastern side of Yellowstone and into this valley has the highest concentration of grizzly bears in the Lower 48.

The rock formations are pretty out of this world too. Features range from the Holy City to the Chimney and the Castle, and there are dozens of others that you can have fun naming yourself. There's one that looks just like Snoopy and another that resembles a wedding cake. Much of the valley is part of the Absaroka Volcanic Field, a 3,000-square-mile area where a series of volcanic rocks are up to 9,000 feet thick.

The scenic byway officially ends at the border of the Shoshone National Forest, but the scenery doesn't end. You'll pass through the Buffalo Bill State Park, the Buffalo Bill Reservoir, Buffalo Bill Dam, and Cedar and Rattlesnake Mountains on your way to Cody. *scenicbyways.info*

The Shoshone National Forest was established in 1891 as part of the Yellowstone Timberland Reserve, making it the country's first national forest. At 2.5 million acres, the Shoshone National Forest is 200,000 acres larger than Yellowstone National Park. The forest has more than 1,300 miles of hiking trails in it and over half of the forest is officially designated as wilderness. In wilderness areas, motorized or mechanized travel or equipment is not allowed. The Shoshone's five wilderness areas are: Washakie, Fitzpatrick, Absaroka-Beartooth, North Absaroka, and Popo Agie Wildernesses. The highest mountain in Wyoming, 13,804-foot Gannett Peak, is in the Shoshone National Forest. *[307] 527-6241, www.fs.usda.gov*

LOCAL LOWDOWN
BOB RICHARD, Retired Yellowstone Park Ranger

Bob Richard's family has guided people into Yellowstone since 1906. In the 1950s, when he was home from college, Bob was Yellowstone's first front-country ranger on horseback.

"I'd ride a horse into a campground and visit with people. [I'd] help them correct things they didn't know they were doing wrong, like dumping waste water out of their trailer," he says. After graduating from college, Bob passed up a full-time job in Yellowstone to become a pilot in the Marine Corps. He went on to fight in the Vietnam War. After the war, he worked as a teacher and school administrator, for the Red Cross in California, and then returned to Cody to found Grub Steak Expeditions, which led visitors into Yellowstone. Bob sold Grub Steak when he was in his 70s. He now fills his time with photography and writing books about the Yellowstone area. His most recent book is *Cody to Yellowstone Beartooth Loop*. Bob has also written a book that is a self-guided photographic tour of the area. *codytoyellowstone.com*

Q: *What's your family's history in the area?*

BOB RICHARD: My grandfather came from Eden, Vermont, at the age of 12. He came out by himself on the railroad to Red Lodge and caught a ride on a wagon to Meeteetse where he went to work for one of the cattle ranches there. In 1908, my granddad was guiding tours into Yellowstone and my grandmother was a guest on one of those trips. When [the tour was over,] she went home to Chicago and my granddad followed her. They married on New Year's Eve in 1908 and then my grandfather brought her back to Cody. On my mom's side, they were cattle and sheep ranchers out of Byron, Wyoming, for about five generations.

NICK COTE

Q: I heard there is an interesting story behind how you met your wife, June. Would you care to share it?

BR: While I was working in the park, I arrested two young nurses from DC for feeding bears. I gave them the option of getting a ticket or going to dinner with a ranger. We went to the Silver Dollar in Jackson. We got back to Yellowstone late that night and the next day we exchanged phone numbers. Three months later, both girls came and got jobs.

Q: Which one became your wife?

BR: I dated the prettiest one, of course! Really, from the first time I saw her, I knew it was June. It was just one of those connections. After June and I got married, her girlfriend went back to DC to get a job that paid more money than Cody did. We had three sons. June died after we had been married for 56 years.

Q: You have quite a photo archive—about 200,000 digital images and another 150,000 on negatives. How'd you get into photography?

BR: When I was in junior high school, my dad started a newspaper called the *Cody Times*. He ended up needing help in the dark room. And then he purchased the [Cody] *Enterprise* and the radio station so he needed more help. If I wasn't [busy with] sports, I was in the community taking photographs for him. Since then, I've continued to keep a camera by my side. I have the files of my life in photographs.

Q: What are your favorite subjects to shoot?

BR: The landscapes in this area and the wildlife. Foremost will be grizzly bears. But I photograph bison the most. They're always there. But any animal, be it the size of a chipmunk or bird, they get my fullest attention.

BUFFALO BILL DAM

Built as a prototype for the Hoover Dam, the Buffalo Bill Dam (actually the Shoshone Dam until 1946 when it was renamed to honor Cody) was the highest dam in the world at 325 feet tall when construction was finished in 1910. The dam was listed on the National Register of Historic Places in 1971 and 2 years later named a National Civil Engineering Landmark. Today it's still impressive and a visitor center helps you understand the engineering behind the structure's magnitude. The dam took 82,900 cubic yards of concrete to make; the last bucket was poured when the temperature was 15 degrees below zero.

In addition to providing irrigation to the Bighorn Basin, the dam created Buffalo Bill Reservoir. Buffalo Bill State Park has camping and fishing areas on the reservoir. Wind blowing down three mountain canyons meets at the reservoir, which is why the reservoir has also been named one of the country's best places to windsurf by *Outside* magazine. *4808 US 14/16/20; (307) 527-6106; BBDVC.com*

↑ Smith Mansion

As gorgeous as the natural scenery is on the road between the East Entrance and Cody, the Smith Mansion will make you pull the car over and stop. The whimsical, pagoda-roofed building, which is part log cabin, part fun house, stands 77 feet tall on a small rise on the south side of the road.

Francis Lee Smith began building the house from fire-damaged lodgepole pine collected from nearby Rattlesnake Mountain without any blueprints in the early 1970s. The Cody native used a crane to raise four heavy timbers into place; that was the only heavy equipment used during construction. His intention was to build a home for his family, and, for a time, the whole family did live there, even though the only electricity came from an extension cord attached to a generator outside. When Smith and his wife, Linda, divorced, he redoubled his efforts and truly let his imagination loose. The house has five floors, more balconies than can be counted, flights of exterior stairs, and a miniature indoor basketball court. The dining table is a massive tree trunk. It does not have anything as prosaic as a bedroom. When Smith's children, Sunny and Bucky, stayed with their dad after the divorce, they'd sometimes

LOCAL LOWDOWN
AMBER KELSEY, Owner of the Beta Coffeehouse

Amber Kelsey's family moved to Cody when she was 3½ years old. Over 30 years later, she's still there. Most days you can find her behind the counter or in the bakery at the Beta Coffeehouse, which she bought in 2016.

Founded in the early 2000s by avid rock climbers Mike and Meg Snyder, the Beta has been through several owners and a move in the last decade. Amber's mission is to make the Beta a positive and loving force in the community. *1450 Sheridan Ave., (307) 587-7707*

ROB WOOD

Q: *Did you know the Beta before you bought it?*

AMBER KELSEY: I've known Meg since we were about 12. I [had] worked for the prior owners for several months, and that's what put me in a position to buy it. But I had to find a new location.

Q: *What's the Beta's role in the community?*

AK: It's one of very few safe, welcoming spaces. We welcome anyone. If you are kind, you belong. I don't allow any hateful actions.

Q: *How has the Cody community changed during your life?*

AK: It used to be a tight-knit, cliquish community, but the younger generation coming up is far more welcoming and cooperative and inclusionary. It's a privilege to see this town realize it has room for everyone.

Q: *What hasn't changed?*

AK: People's independence. The general feel of you do you and I do me and we let each other have space. Also the appreciation of all our wilderness around here.

Q: *What's your favorite coffee drink?*

AK: Honey latte. Honey and coffee are meant for each other. Put a little cinnamon in and it's amazing.

Q: *If someone comes in after a hike, what sweet snack do you recommend?*

AK: We do all of our own baked goods here. We make the best chocolate chip cookies in the world. They are picture perfect—they look like supermodel cookies and they taste as good as they look. We do a killer lavender white chocolate scone too. It is ridiculous.

sleep in sleeping bags next to the wood-burning stove—the only heat source for the entire mansion.

"He was a genius," says Sunny. "Even with everyday things—he just saw them different. He was very eccentric. He was a visionary and an artist in every sense of the word." Smith collected materials such as maple flooring from the Meeteetse high school gym and an elevator from the old Western Wear store in Cody, but he never got around to installing them in his home. We can only speculate as to what he had planned for future additions.

For several years now, Smith's daughter, Sunny Smith Larsen, has been working to preserve the structure via the Smith Mansion Preservation Project. Since Lee's death in 1992 at age 48, the home has fallen prey to vandalism and the elements.

To help raise money to preserve the mansion, Sunny and her husband, Paul, open the house to the public for one weekend a summer. The rest of the year, you'll have to be satisfied with admiring it from the road. *2902 North Fork Hwy./US 14, smithmansion.webnode.com*

CLIMBING IN CODY

Cody is known for having the highest concentration of multipitch ice climbs of anywhere in the Lower 48 states. These climbs are all up the South Fork of the Shoshone. The Cody Ice Fest (*codyicefest.com*) was established in 1998 and has grown into one of the most popular ice-climbing festivals in the country. Joe Josephson, profiled on page 222, wrote the definitive guide to ice climbing in the area, *Winter Dance*.

But Cody isn't just ice climbing. In recent years, the local climbing community has been hard at work on boulder problems on Cedar Mountain. "Bouldering" is rock climbing performed without using ropes or harnesses. (Climbers often place bouldering mats—thick pads—on the ground below them.) A bouldering route, called a "problem," usually gets no more than 20 feet above the ground. About 800 problems at varying levels of difficulty have been identified on sandstone rocks on Cedar Mountain. Coming into Cody from the east, take a right just before you exit the canyon past Buffalo Bill Dam. Go left at the Y junction and continue up the switchbacks. About half of the boulder problems are accessed from the turnout at the end of the third switchback. It's also a nice area to hike around.

ROAD TRIP 2
OLD WEST

In Cody's early days—the town was incorporated in 1901—it wasn't uncommon to see bison running through downtown. Cowboys were known to ride their horses right into the Irma Bar. Co-founded by one of the most popular and well-known personalities of the American West, Buffalo Bill Cody, the town has cleaned up quite a bit since that time, but its heart is still authentically western.

ROB WOOD

NICK COTE

↑ Irma Hotel

In 1883, Buffalo Bill Cody founded his Wild West Show, which went on to tour the country and world for 30 years. You might think he would have been too busy to concern himself with a hotel, but you'd be wrong. It was important to Cody that the town he co-founded have a hotel worthy of the well-to-do Americans and the European royalty who traveled to the area to tour Yellowstone National Park.

Cody hired Lincoln, Nebraska, church architect Alfred Wilderman Woods to design this hotel. Some of the exterior walls are made of local river rock and sandstone from Beck Lake, which is just south of town. The hotel's massive fireplace is constructed from rock, ores, minerals, and even fossils all collected in the Big Horn Basin.

The hotel opened in November 1902 as "The Irma." Cody named it for his 18-year-old daughter. But when he said, "[The Irma] is just the sweetest hotel that ever was," there was no doubt which Irma he was talking about. It was also a fairly lively spot. At the time, tryouts for the Wild West Show were held on lots to the west of the hotel.

If you're planning to overnight in Cody, there is plenty of room at the Irma today. In addition to the original hotel, a northwest annex was built in 1929 and a southwest addition was done in 1977. Or you can hang out in the bar, which is now the Irma's biggest claim to fame. The cherrywood bar is one of the most photographed attractions in the entire town. Queen Victoria gifted it to Buffalo Bill in 1900. Buffalo Bill and Queen Victoria became friends when his Wild West Show traveled to Great Britain. The Queen was taken with Cody's charisma and appreciated that he put on free shows for orphans. The bar was made in France and brought to New York City by steamer. In New York, it was loaded onto a train and then brought to Red Lodge, Montana. From Red Lodge, it took 2 weeks to get it to Cody via horse-pulled freight wagon. *1129 Sheridan Ave., (307) 587-4221, www.irmahotel.com*

↑ Wayne's Boot Shop

Kevin and Kim Lundvall took over running Wayne's Boot Shop on Cody's main street from Kevin's dad, Wayne, in 1996. Wayne had bought the business in 1959, when he was barely 20 years old. He grew up on a ranch in the area and had rheumatic fever as a kid, which damaged his heart valves. "A doctor told him he better find work other than ranching to do," Kevin says. "When he graduated high school, Dad apprenticed at the shoe shop." And then a couple of years later, Wayne bought that shoe repair shop. Wayne fixed boots and shoes in all conditions, but didn't sell any new ones until 1973. Kevin says his dad brought in Nakona boots that year and then "he grew the retail side as he could afford to. He wouldn't borrow money to do it. He added about one new line a year."

Kevin started working in the shop when he was in junior high school. "If we weren't in sports, we were down here tearing shoes apart for dad," he says. "I worked a half-day my senior year in high school. In 1978, I started full time." Kevin has only worked at one other place in his life: "The summer I was sixteen, I worked at a gas station."

Kim didn't start working at Wayne's until her senior year of high school. "My family moved to Cody right before my senior year," she says. "I got a job right away." She remembers her first day vividly. "It was opening day of deer season and Kevin shot a nice whitetail," she says. "He came by the shop to show his folks the deer." At the time, Kevin was running the repair shop part of the business, so Kim began to see him around. "Eventually I started thinking

Kevin was pretty awesome," she says. The two married in July 1985 and Wayne offered Kevin the job of running the repair shop starting that August.

Kim and Kevin took over the whole shebang in 1996. "We signed the papers in February and they left town and went south, which my dad had never done before," Kevin says. "He was able to leave the shop behind. He'd call and check on us, but he was retired, and he loved it." Wayne died in 2014.

Since buying the business, Kim and Kevin have doubled the size of the store, and Kim began keeping the books on a computer. Kevin's "mom did all of the bill pay by hand, so when I took over I decided I was going to do it by computer," Kim says. They have five kids ages 18 to 29. "They have all worked their summers in the shop," Kim says.

The biggest change Kevin and Kim have seen in Cody since they took over ownership of Wayne's Boots is other family businesses disappearing. "I think we're the oldest family business now," Kim says. "Webster's Chevrolet was founded before us, but they sold out a few years ago." *1250 Sheridan Ave., [307] 587-5234, waynesbootshop.com*

NICK COTE

LOCAL LOWDOWN
JAY LINDERMAN, Owner of Adriano's Spaghetti Western

Adriano's is a spaghetti western restaurant of the most authentic sort. Chef Chrissy Linderman specialized in Italian and Mediterranean cuisine while studying at the Culinary Institute of America (Hyde Park, New York, and St. Helena, California). Her husband, Jay, is a former pro rodeo cowboy whose family is pretty much the first family of the sport. Walk into the restaurant, inhale deeply the smell of garlic, and look at the black-and-white photos on the walls of Jay's great uncles (Bud and Bill Linderman are both in the Pro Rodeo Hall of Fame [PRHF]), his dad, Walt, and Walt's world champion horse, Scottie, who was inducted into the PRHF in 2016. You'll even see some photos of Jay. Turn your attention to the menu and you'll find pasta served with Angus steaks. "If you're going to be an Italian restaurant in Cody, Wyoming, you better serve the best steak in town," Jay says. The Aces High Ribeye is served with spaghetti and marinara sauce instead of french fries. "There isn't a baked potato in the house," Jay says. *1244 Sheridan Ave., (307) 527-7320, adrianositalianrestaurant.com*

Q: *You grew up nearby in Belfry, Montana. Did you come to the Cody Nite Rodeo to compete?*

JAY LINDERMAN: That is kind of where I started. I started rodeoing in 1971, maybe 1970, [when] I was a junior in high school. I started bull dogging, following in my dad's footsteps. Every summer, we'd come over to the Cody Nite Show as many times as we could. We'd finish up work and drive here as fast as we could.

Q: *In the 40-some years since, has the Cody rodeo changed?*

JL: It is still kind of the same deal. It is bigger and better managed, but still the same deal.

ROB WOOD

Q: *How'd you go from rodeo to the restaurant business?*

JL: I had a scholarship to Montana State and rodeo-ed through college and then went on to rodeo professionally until 1984. [That was when] I decided I had better go to work for a living. My family has been in rodeo for four generations and they expected me to continue that pursuit. I wasn't really popular with my father when I quit.

Q: *Do you regret quitting?*

JL: Hindsight being 20/20, I would have liked to have pursued rodeo further to see where it would have taken me, but I don't have any regrets having worked. I managed ranches for 30 years before we opened this restaurant.

Q: *What is more difficult: rodeo or running a restaurant?*

JL: Running a restaurant. I was a steer wrestler. With that, the only person you have to worry about is yourself, and I had a young family, so I worried about them too. A restaurant is more of a complicated business.

Q: *Why steer wrestling?*

JL: I was about 220 pounds and that is pretty big for the riding events. I tried those when I was in high school, but my size eventually dictated it was steer wrestling and calf roping.

Q: *What's your favorite item on Adriano's menu?*

JL: I raised black angus cattle for 30 years, so my favorite is the certified angus rib eye steak served with fettuccine alfredo.

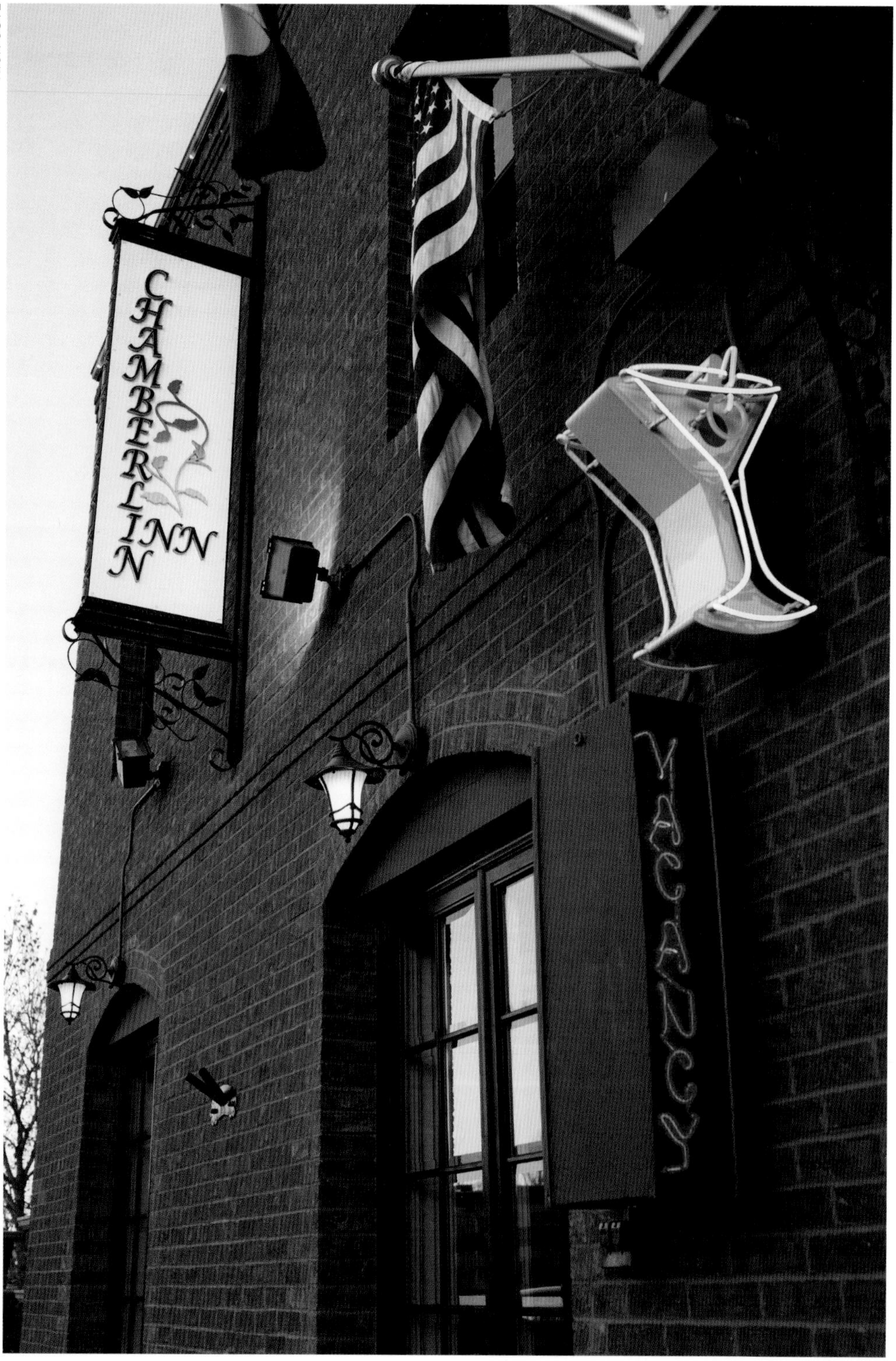

NICK COTE

← Chamberlin Inn

In over a century of continuous operation, the Chamberlin Inn has hosted Ernest Hemingway, Marshall Field, and Erle Halliburton. "In the '20s and '30s, the Chamberlin Inn was the place to stay in Cody," says current owner Ev Diehl.

Agnes Chamberlin opened a simple boardinghouse in 1903 and with her husband's help began adding to it over the years.

Hemingway stayed here in 1932, just after he had completed the manuscript for *Death in the Afternoon*. In between fishing trips on the Clark's Fork River, he mailed the manuscript to his publisher.

While the inn has been in continuous operation since 1903, by the 1980s and 1990s, it had lost much of its luster. In 2005, longtime locals Ev and Susan Diehl bought it and launched a complete renovation. They took the claw-foot tubs that could be salvaged and sent them up to Billings to be re-enameled. They pulled the original steam radiators out of all of the rooms and sandblasted "about thirty coats of paint" off them, says Ev, before re-installing

them. They pulled fake paneling off of walls and demolished dropped ceilings. They chipped off plaster applied over original brick walls.

The Diehls are the first ones to point out that they remodeled the place rather than renovated it. "We kept as much of the original stuff as we could, but before, the interior was all heads and horns," Ev says. "I had spent 8 years at the [Buffalo Bill Center of the West] and was tired of that look. We went with an art nouveau theme instead, which was a look at that time." The Chamberlin has twenty-one rooms in three different historic buildings. The public lounge, Chamberlin Spirits, serves wine and cocktails. Also, "we encourage anyone to stop in. We love giving tours," Ev says. "If rooms aren't occupied, we leave all of the doors open." *1032 12th St., (307) 587-0202, chamberlininn.com*

⬇ Dug Up Gun Museum

Guns can be expensive to collect. Especially when you're 8 years old. But if a gun is rusted, ruined, or jammed, it's a lot cheaper. So that's what young Hans Kurth started collecting. "It was a way to collect all of these models of guns I couldn't afford in any other condition," Kurth says.

By the time he was old enough to afford guns in better condition, Kurth was hooked on the busted ones. "They get your imagination going," he says.

ROB WOOD

"They're living history. These aren't the guns that spent their lives in a box in a desk drawer. These were the guns that paved the way for us to travel west and do things that are often taken for granted now. These guns and people paved the way and sometimes paid the price." For example: Kurth's collection includes several guns that are half loaded or cocked and half loaded. "That's not a good sign," he says. "You don't have to be a CSI guy to figure out what happened."

Kurth and his wife, Eva, opened the Dug Up Gun Museum in Cody in 2009 with about 900 guns and artifacts on display. Since opening, several hundred guns have been added to the collection. And Kurth says he has even more, but he's holding them back until he has a better idea of their history. "I never want to sell an item short, so I really want to do as much research as I can."

The museum has an 1873 Colt single-action Army revolver that was found in 1971 in an old mining payroll office in Price, Utah. Kurth's research indicates that it is possible this gun belonged to Butch Cassidy. In the late 1890s, Cassidy and a compatriot (not the Sundance Kid) robbed the payroll office. During the robbery, Cassidy and his partner got away with $9,980 in silver

LOCAL LOWDOWN

DAN MILLER, Owner of Dan Miller's Cowboy Music Revue

The first time Dan Miller sang on stage, he was 8 or 9, and the stage was near the Indiana dairy farm he grew up on. The first time his youngest daughter, Hannah, performed on stage, she was 6. That stage was in Cody, Wyoming, and the show was Dan Miller's Cowboy Music Revue. Hannah is now in college, and, despite Dan's own successful music and broadcast career in Nashville (and Cody), "it's gotten to the point where I'm Hannah's dad and not Dan Miller," he says. "But I love it. I absolutely love it. I'm very proud. Our favorite daddy/daughter thing to do is play music."

While Hannah's career is yet to be determined, Dan's is still in full swing. Monday through Saturday from June 1 through September 30, he headlines the Cowboy Music Revue at the Buffalo Bill Center of the West. Since founding the show in 2005, Miller's group has performed more than 1,400 shows together. When not performing in Cody, Miller produces and hosts television programming including *Xtreme Bulls* and *Best of the West*. It is his live performances that are closest to his heart though. *720 Sheridan Ave., (307) 578-7909, cowboymusicreview.com*

Q: *How'd you get into music?*

DAN MILLER: I think I grew up doing the typical things, and started in bands when I was pretty young.

Q: *How'd you get from local bands to Nashville?*

DM: I went to college on a football scholarship and after college I went to L.A. In the early days, it was the Dan Miller Band and we'd play Vegas, Reno, Tahoe wearing tuxedos and playing lounges and showrooms. It was always country music that was in my soul though. In the mid-1980s, the Nashville Network was just coming online. I thought Nashville might be the best of both worlds, so I went there and started auditioning for everything. I've hosted more Nashville Network shows than anyone else.

Q: *What brought you to Cody?*

DM: I love Cody for its proximity to Yellowstone and also because of Wyoming's public school system. My daughters have both

gone through that system. And I just thought it was a nice place to raise a family.

Q: How do you keep the music review fresh for you and the group?

DM: I never do the same show twice in a row. There is always some spontaneity and that makes it fun. My goal with every show is for us to enjoy it as much as the audience does.

Q: There are a lot of variations to choose from in country music. Why'd you decide on a program of the genre's classics?

DM: My thought was that people were in Wyoming looking for an authentic western experience. So we do Sons of the Pioneers, "Tumbling Tumbleweeds," "Cool Water"–Roy Rogers–type stuff. People remember those songs from their childhood. I'll do some cowboy poetry. There's also some Asleep at the Wheel though–it is a real variety.

Q: Sometimes you bring Nashville friends–the Bellamy Brothers, Kathy Mattea, Billy Dean, Asleep at the Wheel, Gary Morris–out to play in Cody. What do they think of the area?

DM: Every single one wants to come back. Gary [Morris] would rather fly fish than sing.

and gold, but Cassidy dropped his gun and it fell through the floorboards. It's believed that the gun sat beneath the floorboards until it was found in 1971. "There's no way to say for sure that this is that gun, but it is certainly the exact type of gun Butch is known to have used," Kurth says.

There's also the loaded Colt that was pulled from muck in the Meramec River in St. Louis in the summer of 1971. A family on a rafting trip spotted the gun and called the police. The sheriff came and retrieved it, then took it back to the sheriff's office where he washed it off. Once it was cleaned, he couldn't find a serial number, but could tell it was a Colt, and that it was loaded. For 30-some years, it sat in the sheriff's office. When the deputy that retrieved it retired, it was given to him as a going away present. "He came into the museum one summer and said, 'I got something for you,'" Kurth says. "And then he mailed it to us. He and I both know that somehow, someway that this was some type of crime gun. The gun dates from the early 1920s. St. Louis did have quite a history with the Mob in that time period."

And then there is the musket that was found in the fork of a madrone tree in California. The tree had grown around the musket. "There are a thousand stories you could come up with about that one," Kurth says.

Included in the museum's collection are pistols, revolvers, muskets, and rifles dating from the Civil War to World War II. The museum is open May through September. *1020 12th St., [307] 587-3344, www.codydugupgun museum.com*

THOMAS MOLESWORTH

Thomas Molesworth is known as the godfather of ranch-style furniture. Trained at the Art Institute of Chicago, Molesworth moved to Cody with his wife in 1931 and opened his own furniture business. He developed a distinctly western style of furniture that was inspired by the Arts and Crafts style but used natural wood, antlers, and hides. A 1940s Molesworth sofa recently sold at auction for $50,000. A 1930s club chair went for $25,000. Several original Molesworth pieces are in the collection of the Buffalo Bill Center of the West. Vintage Molesworth furniture and accessories are a big deal, and they were all made at his workshop in Cody.

LOCAL LOWDOWN
LESTER SANTOS, Furniture Maker

Lester Santos's furniture has been featured on the *Today* show, on the Home and Garden Network, and in *Architectural Digest*. Clients from across the county find him despite the fact, "I don't advertise anywhere," he says. A piece of his—a phantasmagorical desk made from burled juniper, cherry, copper, rosewood, and stained glass—is in the permanent collection of the Buffalo Bill Center of the West. Still, the thing Santos is most proud of professionally is not a piece of furniture. That honor goes to a guitar he made in the mid-1970s while working at the now-defunct NBN Guitars. *santosfurniture.com*

ROB WOOD

Q: *What's so special about this guitar?*

LESTER SANTOS: It was the last guitar we built before we went out of business. We gave it to Elvis Presley right before he played in Denver. I think we were kind of hoping he would ride in and save the company. Recently, I saw it on the auction channel and it sold for $42,000.

Q: *So Elvis never rode in and saved NBN?*

LS: No, but he used the guitar when he played his Denver show.

Q: *How'd you get into furniture building?*

LS: Around 1971, I answered an ad in the paper in New Bedford, Massachusetts. A harpsichord builder was looking for an apprentice. I learned how to understand wood and tools. We didn't have any electricity in the shop—there were huge windows with natural light. We did everything by hand—it was the best way to learn. I learned how to put wood together so it won't come apart. No one teaches that anymore.

Q: *And then you went on to make guitars?*

LS: I was a musician beginning at age 13. A friend of mine had moved to Boulder [Colorado] and sent me a local paper where NBN was hiring. I moved from Dartmouth, Massachusetts, to work for these two brothers. But in 1976 and 1977, Japanese imports started flooding the American market and that just killed us.

Q: *How did you end up in Cody?*

LS: My neighbor in Colorado and I started a band, Button Fly. We ended up playing all over the Rocky Mountain West, including Cody. We did Top 40, country, a few originals—kind of Jimmy Buffett/Eagles style of music. I eventually got tired of all that and found myself in Cody. I started doing some remodeling and making kitchen cabinets. I had one project that was Molesworth revival and that got me hooked on making this western furniture.

Q: *How would you describe your style?*

LS: I'd say there is a Molesworth inspiration. I fall back on it as something that is easy for me to do and it is popular, but what I really like to do is take rustic and mix it with art deco. It's just a little different.

◆ ROAD TRIP 3
CULTURE

Perhaps more than any one thing, Cody is known as being home to the Buffalo Bill Center of the West (BBCW) (formerly the Buffalo Bill Historic Center). This western-centric, mega museum has been called "the Smithsonian of the West." But that doesn't do it justice. As high as your expectations for the BBCW are, it will exceed them. While the BBCW celebrates (mostly) the positives of the American West, a newer museum in the area, the Heart Mountain Interpretive Center, takes a closer look at a low moment in the country's history.

← Buffalo Bill Center of the West

Buffalo Bill's niece Mary Jester Allen spearheaded the founding of a museum celebrating her uncle. The Buffalo Bill Museum opened in 1927, adjacent to the 12-foot-tall bronze sculpture titled *Buffalo Bill—The Scout* by Gertrude Vanderbilt Whitney that had been unveiled 3 years earlier. (In addition to being a sculptor, Whitney was also a prodigious supporter and collector of art; she's the same Whitney who, in 1930, founded the Whitney American Art Museum in New York.) In 1959, the Whitney Gallery of Western Art opened. (Whitney donated the land it was built on.) In 1969, the Buffalo Bill Museum moved into a bigger space closer to the Whitney Gallery. (The original museum still stands; today it's the Cody Country Chamber of Commerce.) In 1976, the Cody Firearms Museum opened. Three years later came the Plains Indian Museum. The McCracken Research Library followed in 1980. In June 2002, the Draper Natural History Museum opened (with Clint Eastwood in attendance).

LOCAL LOWDOWN
ASHLEY HLEBINSKY, Curator of the Cody Firearms Museum

"There are lots of people who end up wandering in here and have no interest in firearms; they just come in because they're already at the center," says Ashley Hlebinsky, Robert W. Woodruff Curator at the Cody Firearms

ROB WOOD

Museum. "And they'll still be here 3 hours later. They're awestruck."

You do not need to be a gun person to appreciate the artistry and history of the firearms museum's extensive collection—only about 4,000 of the 7,000 pieces in the collection are currently on display. Take the Lincoln-Head Hammer Gun. Sharpshooter and gunsmith Hiram Berdan made this breech-loading percussion rifle in 1863 to honor President Lincoln, who was known to have an interest in firearm technology. Instead of a traditional hammer, this rifle has a portrait bust of Lincoln as its hammer. "It was never given to Lincoln though," Hleblinsky says. "He was assassinated before that could happen."

The museum also has dozens of Hollywood guns and artifacts, including a revolver believed to have been used in *High Noon*, guns from the show *Bonanza*, a *Gunsmoke* gun, and several original *Gunsmoke* scripts.

Hlebinsky did not grow up around guns. She grew up wanting to be a doctor and was interested in the history of medicine, specifically battlefield medicine. When she was 18, she did a Civil War medicine tour at Gettysburg. Part of the tour covered how the advancement of weapon technology changed medical technology. "Before that I had never thought about firearms in my life," she says. "It was then that I decided to study history." Hlebinsky soon landed an internship at a military museum in Pittsburgh. "They put 200 guns in front of me, from the Civil War to one that belonged to an Iraq War veteran and I got totally hooked on the technology side of it and the diversity of firearms." When getting her master's degree in American history and museum studies, she focused on the perception of firearms in culture. *720 Sheridan Ave., (307) 587–4771, centerofthewest.org/explore/firearms*

Q: *Do you have your own gun collection?*

ASHLEY HLEBINSKY: A little one. According to the curator's code of ethics, you cannot collect what you curate. Following the code, if you are at a gun show and you have the option to buy a historic piece, you should buy it for the museum before you buy it for yourself. The nice thing about managing a collection of 7,000 firearms is that anything I can afford, we already have many of. But I have some historic pieces I bought when I first started studying firearms. Now I prefer to play with the ones I don't have to pay for.

Q: *Do you just study guns, or have you started shooting?*

AH: I've taken NRA courses and learned to shoot historic and modern guns. I'm an NRA-certified instructor too. I taught my dad to shoot about 2 years ago. When I took my NRA basic pistol course, I did that with my mom.

Q: *You're not yet 30 and you're already curator of what is arguably the finest firearms museum in the country. Not that you're looking at leaving, but where would you go from here?*

AH: Probably into consulting. Most museums have at least one gun in their collection but don't have staff that know how to interpret it. Being a firearms curator is a unique thing. There are people who study guns and people who do museum studies; not many people study both.

Q: *What do you mean when you say "interpret" a gun?*

AH: Here we interpret military history, western history, hunting and conservation, embellishment history–all through the lens of firearms. Ours is the only [museum at the BBCW] with a mission that goes beyond the American West. Our collection dates back to the 1400s and has international pieces. It's an encyclopedic collection.

JUST SAYIN'

A few common American sayings that owe their origins to firearms. "A" is the original definition, and "B" is the modern meaning.

Bite the bullet:
A. Prior to modern medical care, a wounded person was given a lead bullet to bite down on while undergoing surgery to lessen the pain.
B. To do something unpleasant in order to get it out of the way.

Flash in the pan:
A. When a flintlock's priming pan powder burns, or "flashes," but fails to ignite the main powder charge in the barrel.
B. A person who claims great skills or achievements but accomplishes nothing.

Going off half-cocked:
A. Placing the hammer of a firearm on a half-way position so that it is unable to be fired.
B. Thoughtless or hasty behavior.

Buffalo Bill started working at the age of 11. By 14, he was a rider for the Pony Express. During an 18-month period when he was in his early 20s, he killed an estimated 4,280 bison to feed the Army and Kansas Pacific Railroad. He founded his famous Wild West Show when he was in his mid-30s. The town of Cody was incorporated when Buffalo Bill was 55. Buffalo Bill died when he was 70.

Together, these five museums and research library total 300,000 square feet of displays and exhibitions, larger than five football fields put together. Displays include a lock of Buffalo Bill's hair; a costume worn in the Wild West Show by Annie Oakley; Bear 104, a grizzly often seen on US 14 between Cody and Yellowstone that was eventually killed by a car; paintings by Charles Russell; 16th-century dueling pistols; and, seasonally, the Draper Museum Raptor Experience, which allows guests to see real-life birds of prey like a golden eagle, great horned owl, and American kestrel. The center is an affiliate of the Smithsonian. *720 Sheridan Ave., (307) 587-4771, centerofthewest.org*

McCracken Research Library

When you've got the Buffalo Bill Museum, Plains Indian Museum, Whitney Western Art Museum, Cody Firearms Museum, and the Draper Natural History Museum all under one roof, it'd be understandable to overlook the McCracken Research Library. Especially since seeing most of the items in the library's collection requires an advance appointment. The library has a small, no-appointment-necessary gallery with changing exhibits that "show what the library is about," says library director Mary Robinson. When the National Park Service celebrated its centennial in 2016, the display in the library gallery was of early Yellowstone photographs. But you can't just waltz into the library's stacks, which house nearly 450 manuscript collections, 750,000 images, and more than 30,000 books. The library's collection is worth advance planning and making an appointment for though.

Included in the McCracken's vaults is one of the few complete sets of Edward Curtis's *The North American Indian.* "This is one of the treasures of Americana and ours is in great condition," Mary says. And, if you make an appointment, you can see it.

Curtis published *The North American Indian* between 1907 and 1930. In total, the collection includes twenty folios, containing over 700 photographs, and twenty text volumes that contain over 1,500 smaller photographs. (Curtis took more than 40,000 images of Native Americans in eighty different tribes.) Curtis also recorded tribes' oral histories and took notes on traditional foods, clothing, and ceremonies. In 2012, a complete *North American Indian* sold at auction for $1.44 million.

While Curtis's magnum opus is one of the library's stars, Mary says she enjoys the journals and letters of regular people the library has. "They are just wonderful and fascinating," she says. "Some of my favorites you can even go online and read, they are transcribed and are letters from Victor Arland in French to a compatriot." The letters cover Arland's attempt to set up an establishment in the Cody area, trading with Indians, and fights between drunken cowboys. "It is a wonderful window into living on the frontier," Mary says. "People don't usually come here for the library, but sometimes it's why they stay." *720 Sheridan Ave., (307) 587-4771, centerofthewest.org/research/ mccracken-research-library*

↓ Heart Mountain

During the time Heart Mountain Relocation Center operated outside of Cody—from August 1942 to November 1945—its population of about 10,700 Japanese-American internees was nearly five times that of Cody itself. Casper and Cheyenne were the only cities in Wyoming that had bigger populations than Heart Mountain.

DAVID KRAUSE

HEART MOUNTAIN MOVEMENT

Heart Mountain is easy to spot, sitting by itself north of Cody. It wasn't always that way though. Some 50 million years ago, it was part of the Absaroka Range, the foothills of which are nearly two dozen miles away. How it got to its present location is a matter of earnest debate. Some scientists surmise that a series of seriously strange geologic events—volcanic eruptions, lava trapped underground, water filling underground dikes—lifted the mountain and moved it 62 miles east.

The hike to the 8,123-foot summit of Heart Mountain is about 8 miles round-trip. Start it at the Heart Mountain Ranch, which belongs to The Nature Conservancy. At the trailhead, find a cabin originally built in 1884 and recently restored. Operated in conjunction with the Buffalo Bill Center of the West, the cabin has information about the geology, cultural significance, and ecology of the mountain and the surrounding land. *1357 Rd. 22, (307) 754-8446, www.nature.org*

Of course the Heart Mountain camp wasn't truly the state's third-largest city. Nine guard towers joined by a barbed wire fence kept watch over the 467 barrack-style buildings. The Japanese-American doctors who worked in the camp's 150-bed hospital made $19 per month, while the Caucasian nurses who worked there made $150 a month. Internees were given a loyalty questionnaire and were prohibited from voting. The last Heart Mountain incarcerees left in November 1945; they were given $25 and a train ticket to anywhere in the United States.

While most of the camp's buildings are long gone, a few remain: a hospital boiler house and its attached red brick chimney; two hospital buildings; an administrative building; the high school's concrete vault; a root cellar; and a huge hole that served as the camp's swimming pool. If you drive along WY 14A, you can see former barracks repurposed as storage sheds and barns.

After many years of fund-raising, the Heart Mountain Foundation opened Heart Mountain Interpretive Center in 2011. This museum uses interactive exhibits, artifacts, photographs, and oral histories to show what life was like for the 14,000 people imprisoned there, most brought to the camp from the West Coast, over its 3-year existence.

Though Heart Mountain was a prison camp, you might be surprised to learn that it had thirteen Boy Scout troops and one Girl Scout troop. Or that

its high school football team, the Heart Mountain Eagles, lost only one game in its 2 years of competing against area schools. The *Heart Mountain Sentinel* published its first edition in October 1942 and was published every Saturday thereafter until the camp closed. There were knitting and flower-arranging groups for adults and dances for teens. *1539 Rd. 19, Powell, (307) 754-8000, heartmountain.org*

EXIT

◆ ROAD TRIP 4
HOT SPRINGS AND MEETEETSE

When Wyoming families are looking for a vacation close to home, Thermop-olis, the seat of Hot Springs County, is often their destination. Size-wise, Hot Springs County is the smallest county in Wyoming (with fewer than 5,000 residents, it's the second least populous) and came into being only when neighboring counties decided they really didn't want this land. So Hot Springs County was born. While ranching and farming around here is indeed difficult, the one-stoplight town of Thermopolis is locally famous for its mineral hot springs. There is also a dinosaur center. Between Cody and "Thermop" (go ahead and use the local lingo) in Meeteetse, you'll be surprised to find what might be the best chocolate truffles you've ever had.

⬇ The Hot Spring State Park Bison Herd

In 2016, the Hot Springs State Park bison herd, which is the central herd for the Wyoming State Park system, celebrated its one hundredth anniversary. In 1916, a bull was captured in Yellowstone National Park and brought to the state park. Several heifers were purchased from a ranch in Kansas and brought to Thermopolis. Since these founding members of the herd were established here, no additional outside bison have been brought in. "We've never strayed from the genetics," says Hot Springs State Park superinten-dent Kevin Skates. "Since this herd is quite isolated, we don't have problems with diseases or things like that."

The size of the herd depends on the condition of the park's pasture. The herd usually numbers between one and two dozen animals. When the herd gets bigger than the park's pasture can support, it sells calves and yearlings off. In early 2017, the park auctioned off nine calves and yearlings. Interested in owning a bison? The sale has happened annually for at least 50 years. Bidding usually opens in late December and closes in early to mid-January. All bidding is done silently, whether online or via mail. The minimum bid for a yearling bull is $2,000 and $1,800 for a calf. The highest bidder wins. "Peo-ple like to buy our animals," Skates says. "I'd say 90 percent of bids come from ranchers looking to buy them to add to their herd." But there are no

LOCAL LOWDOWN

KEVIN SKATES, Superintendent, Hot Springs State Park

Kevin Skates moved to Thermopolis to work as Hot Springs State Park's (HSSP) superintendent in 2005. Before that, he was in Rawlins, in the south-central part of the state. Today, in addition to being responsible for HSSP, where there are hot springs, a herd of bison, several miles of hiking trails, and what are arguably the state park system's best flower gardens, Skates is also in charge of the Legend Rock Petroglyph Site, where rock art dates back more than 11,000 years.

Q: *What's a typical day look like for you?*

KEVIN SKATES: We're the busiest of all the state parks–48 percent of visitation to state parks is through us.

Q: *It sounds like maybe you should take some time to soak more often.*

KS: You're right! Since we're located right in town, it's almost like we're a city park. All of the people in Thermopolis think it's the town park. We have nineteen leases in the

COURTESY HOT SPRINGS STATE PARK

184

park–from the hospital to the high school, the fairgrounds, the county library, the senior center–sometimes it seems like everything is located in the state park. I think it's kind of the economic engine that drives the community. The park defines the town and there's a lot of ownership in the park from the local community.

Q: *Are most soakers locals or visitors?*

KS: In the summer, I'd say it's 90 percent visitors soaking. In the winter, it's probably only 50 percent visitors.

Q: *Is there any truth to the claim, written out in giant white letters on the side of Monument Hill, that these are the "world's largest mineral hot springs"?*

KS: As far as I can tell, that claim started in the 1940s as a way to advertise the place. Are we the world's largest? Probably not. But we are still unique. The mineral content in the water here is so high. It was always called "the healing waters" and for decades people came here for medicinal reasons. That's why the hospital is right here. There used to be several sanitariums; people would come for weeks or months.

Q: *Do you have to do anything to the water to make it safe for soaking?*

KS: No. We don't filter it or put any chemicals in it. It naturally has a lot of chloride in it.

HOT SPRINGS STATE PARK

requirements for bidders. Occasionally the park has auctioned off a 2- or 3-year-old bison. "Someone might buy one of these to butcher," Skates says.

While the bison are often visible throughout the day, you can guarantee seeing them if you come when they're being fed their daily supplemental "cake" with vitamins and minerals they might not get from the park's natural forage. This happens between 8 and 9 a.m.

Wyoming Dinosaur Center

"Jimbo," one of the largest dinosaurs ever mounted, lives at Thermopolis's Wyoming Dinosaur Center. He lives in the private facility on the edge of town with more than thirty friends, including Stan, a 35-foot T-Rex, a duck-billed Maiasaura, a Triceratops, and a 150-million-year-old Archaeopteryx fossil.

The latter is one of only ten such fossils in the world and the only one outside of Europe. Understandably it is kept beneath bulletproof glass.

While wandering the museum, you can watch paleontologists at work in addition to getting up close and personal with these prehistoric Wyoming residents. Jimbo, who is 106 feet long, was discovered about 3 hours away outside of Douglas, Wyoming.

Between May and September, you can go out with center paleontologists on a real dinosaur dig. The "Dig For A Day" program is open to all ages; children under the age of 18 must be accompanied by an adult. The Wyoming Dinosaur Center is one of the few dino museums in the world to have excavation sites within driving distance. There are approximately 130 dig sites—only about twenty are active—on the nearby 7,700-acre Warm Springs Ranch, which the center owns.

Former Swiss veterinarian Burkhard Pohl vacationed in the area in 1993 and, with friends, found the first dinosaur bones on Warm Springs Ranch. An amateur fossil hunter, Pohl went on to buy the ranch and create the Wyoming Dinosaur Center. Since then, more than 10,000 bones have been discovered and removed from excavation sites on the ranch.

Most fossils found are from sauropods, a class of dinosaurs that lived roughly 65 to 150 million years ago. Camarasaurus, Diplodocus, Camptosaurus, and Apatosaurus are all sauropods. Defining features of the class are long tails and necks and small heads. Sauropods are the largest animals to have ever lived on land. [307] 864-2997, 110 Carter Ranch Rd., wyodino.org

State Bath House

The natural mineral water that flows from the Hot Springs State Park's spring is funneled to five different pools: at the Best Western, at the Days Inn, the Star Plunge, Tepee Pools, and the pool at the State Bath House. Only one of these five is free to use: the State Bath House. While the State Bath House doesn't have water slides like the Star Plunge or Tepee and it might be more crowded than the guests-only pools at the Best Western and the Days Inn, it has the most history, going all the way back to the great Shoshone warrior Chief Washakie.

The land that is today the state park was once part of the Wind River Indian Reservation. In 1897, Chief Washakie sold a 100-square-mile parcel of the reservation to the United States for $60,000 and a promise. The promise the chief exacted? A portion of the hot springs there had to be reserved for free public use. (A pageant celebrating this gift from the Shoshone tribe is held in Thermopolis annually every first weekend in August.) While various state and federal government entities aren't known for keeping promises made to Native Americans, this promise has been kept in the form of the State Bath House.

The current State Bath House dates to 1966. There were three State Bath Houses prior to that; the first one opened in 1900. "For over 100 years now, we've honored the treaty," says park superintendent Kevin Skates. "If someone comes to town, they can soak and not pay a fee." While soaking at the Bath House is free, there's a nominal fee to rent a towel and/or swimsuit. Water is kept at 104 degrees. *538 N. Park St., Thermopolis, [307] 864-2176, wyoparks.state.wy.us*

↓ Safari Club's Taxidermy Collection

Over 300 heads and hides hang on the walls of the Safari Club restaurant inside the Days Inn. The bulk of the animals were shot and killed by former owner Jim Mills. The mounts not killed by Mills were likely killed by his father, who started the collection in the 1950s. Jim Mills went on nearly two dozen African safaris. His first time hunting in Africa was in the 1960s when he was

SAFARI CLUB

28. On that trip, he killed the "big five"—elephant, rhinoceros, water buffalo, lion, and leopard. Mills repeated this feat on several subsequent safaris. One rhino on display was not killed by Mills or his father. It was not killed at all. By the time Mills shot this rhino in Namibia, the species was endangered, so this is a replica. Mills switched from hunting with a rifle to hunting with a bow and arrow so he could "catch and release." He shot this rhino with an arrow armed with a dart and a serum that temporarily put it to sleep. After a model of the rhino was made, antidote to the sleeping serum was administered. The rhino quickly woke up and took off. In addition to the replica rhino, the collection includes marlins, zebra, bears, cheetahs, tigers, lions, alligator, elk, elephant, and mid-Asian ibex. *(307) 864-3131, 115 E. Park St., thermopolisdaysinn.com*

↓ Legend Rocks State Petroglyph Site

One of the largest petroglyph sites in the United States, Legend Rock Petroglyph Site is off WY 120 between Meeteetse and Thermopolis. Archaeologists have counted more than 300 petroglyphs carved into a sheltered, 400-meter-long cliff face. In 1913, the US Geological Survey "discovered" and

KYLE BURNS

LOCAL LOWDOWN
TIM KELLOGG, the Meeteetse Chocolatier

Rosemary caramels; yuzu caramels; rosemary, olive oil, and sea salt truffles—these are the flavors chocolatier Tim Kellogg is excited about now. His grandmother's recipes were the initial inspiration behind his foray into chocolatiering. Kellogg, a cowboy and competitive bronco rider, only started selling truffles to fund his rodeoing. What would grandma think of Kellogg's exotic flavor combinations? He says: "She would probably be a little suspect at first, but I think she'd try them and love them. She was adventurous with her cooking from time to time. I think she'd appreciate I was being adventurous, too."

It was only around 2010, after a fairly significant rodeo injury, that Kellogg committed to making chocolate. "I realized I couldn't work full time on a ranch, run a business, and also rodeo," he says. "One had to go." He wasn't about to give up the ranch work. The plan was to recover from his injuries and then decide between chocolate and rodeo. When the time came, the decision was obvious, but not easy. "I knew I was never going to get to the NFR [National Finals Rodeo] or make a living off of it," he says. "But mentally it was hard on me to stop."

While Kellogg gave up rodeo, he worked on the ranch through 2015 and only left because it sold and the new owners brought in their own people. As successful as his shop is now, Kellogg hopes for a new ranch gig. "I need cattle in my life," he says. But, as committed as he is to cowboying and to chocolate, please don't call Kellogg the cowboy chocolatier. "I didn't ever want the cowboy aspect to be a gimmick. I think my skills on the ranch and my skills in the shop speak for themselves. I work very hard."

MEETEETSE CHOCOLATIER'S SAGE TRUFFLE

Eighty-seven species of mammals, ninety-four bird species, and twelve species of grasshoppers depend on the thirteen different species of sagebrush that grow in Wyoming. Thousands of chocolate fans across the country (and around the world) depend on the sage that chocolatier Tim Kellogg uses in his sage truffles. Even though Wyoming has more sage than almost any other state, Kellogg has to buy culinary sage to use in his chocolates. Kellogg opened Meeteetse Chocolatier, an artisan chocolate store, in downtown Meeteetse in 2003. Then in 2015, he opened a much smaller outpost in Jackson. In addition to sage truffles, Kellogg makes truffles infused with huckleberry, Wyoming Whiskey, and even Coors beer. Right now, he's doing "a lot with caramel," he says. He makes every single truffle and caramel himself, by hand. *Meeteetse: (307) 868-2567, 1943 State St.; Jackson: (307) 413-8296, 265 W. Broadway; www.meeteetse chocolatier.com*

documented the site. In 1973, it was listed on the National Register of Historic Places. In 1988, archaeologists used radiocarbon, cation-ratio, and varnish micro-lamination dating techniques to determine the age of the images. Some were found to be more than 11,000 years old.

Despite the importance of this site, until 2011, there were no signs directing visitors to it and visiting it had to be planned well in advance: You had to pick up a key to Legend Rock's entrance gate from one of several spots in Thermopolis (the State Bath House, the Thermopolis Chamber of Commerce, or the Hot Springs County Museum). In 2011, a visitor center was built. Volunteers staff it daily from 8 a.m. to 6 p.m. between May and September. Between October and April, the site is accessible, but you need to stop at one of the three places mentioned above to get a key for the gate. *[307] 864-2176, wyoparks.state.wy.us*

AMELIA EARHART

Entering Meeteetse from the north, you might see a small memorial to Amelia Earhart. Why? The aviatrix planned on retiring to a spot near the former mining area of Kirwin, in the Shoshone National Forest southwest of Meeteetse.

In 1934, Earhart and husband, George Putnam, went on a 2-week pack trip into the nearby mountains with Carl Dunrud, an area outfitter who also ran the Double Dee Ranch. She loved the area, bought land, and chatted with Dunrud about building her a small cabin. When she and navigator Fred Noonan disappeared over the Pacific in July 1937, Dunrud had already started construction on a simple log cabin for her. Before she took off on her flight around the world, Earhart sent Dunrud a couple of personal items, including a flight jacket and buffalo coat gifted her by actor William Hart, to store until the cabin was finished. After her death, Dunrud donated these to the Buffalo Bill Center of the West, where they are still in the permanent collection.

ROAD TRIP 5
WILD LANDS

Just because you leave Yellowstone National Park doesn't mean you leave behind natural beauty and geological superlatives. Outside of the park's East Entrance is the largest mountain mass in the entire Greater Yellowstone Ecosystem, the country's first wild horse preserve, Wyoming's only Wild and Scenic designated river, and the Grand Canyon of the North.

South Fork

The North Fork Highway, aka US 14/16/20, is a designated National Scenic Byway, the Buffalo Bill Scenic Byway, and also a Wyoming Scenic Byway. It's a gorgeous drive. Its counterpart, South Fork Road, aka WY 291, is just as

stunningly beautiful, and it's much less crowded. Any traffic jams are caused by hay trucks or cattle drives. The South Fork Valley is the heart of Cody's cattle country.

While the North Fork Highway parallels the North Fork of the Shoshone River for much of its length, the South Fork Road meanders alongside the South Fork of the Shoshone. The North Fork Highway takes you to the East Entrance of Yellowstone National Park. South Fork Road dead-ends at a trail-head from which you can hike to the spot farthest from a paved road in the Lower 48 states (the Thorofare region of Yellowstone).

South Fork Road starts on the west side of Cody and goes for about 40 miles before it ends. Along the way, you'll pass the former farms of German settlers brought to the South Fork Valley in the early 1900s by Buffalo Bill himself—he even paid for their train tickets from New York. Some of these farms are still worked by the descendants of those immigrants.

You'll also travel parallel to Carter Mountain. At 12,319 feet tall and 30 miles wide, it is the largest mountain mass in the entire Greater Yellowstone

Ecosystem. Next comes Castle Rock, the unofficial divide between the upper and lower South Fork Valley. Native Americans called this feature *Ishawooa*, which means "rock in the valley." While Castle Rock is no longer known by this name, a creek at the southern end of the valley has been named Ishawooa. About 35 miles down the road, you'll pass the TE Ranch, Buffalo Bill's former ranch and hunting retreat. Just before the road ends at Cabin Creek, you'll hit Deer Creek Campground. If you can't spend the night, it makes a great picnic spot.

Pryor Mountain Wild Horses

Horses have lived wild on Pryor Mountain straddling the Wyoming-Montana border for a couple of centuries. But it wasn't until 1968 that any federal protection was given to them. That year, US secretary of the interior Stewart Udall created the country's first wild horse range, the 31,000-acre Pryor Mountain Wild Horse Range. The range was later expanded to 38,000 acres, but the horses are truly free to roam; there are no fences to keep them from wandering into adjacent national forest land. The Pryor Mountain horses are the only wild horses in the state of Montana, and the herd usually numbers around 160. The larger herd separates into smaller groups called "harems" with one stallion as the leader of the mares and younger horses.

The best spot to see bands of these horses is along WY 37 in the Bighorn Canyon National Recreation Area. The company Pryor Wild does guided, daylong trips to view and photograph the horses. Founded by longtime Lovell locals Steve and Nancy Cerroni, Pryor Wild takes clients up Burnt Timber Ridge Road, which climbs 4,400 feet over 12 bumpy miles. At the top, expect to see wildflowers in addition to horses. If you want to horse-watch on your own, first stop at the Pryor Mountain Wild Mustang Center. They'll have reports on where horses have most recently been spotted. They've also adopted some horses from the herd over the years.

The Bureau of Land Management, which has jurisdiction over the range, asks that you stay more than 100 feet from the wild horses and never feed them. You can get as close as you'd like to the adopted horses at the center though. Bring the herd into your own home by watching the 1995 documentary film *Cloud: Wild Stallion of the Rockies* and its sequel, the 2003 documentary *Cloud's Legacy: The Wild Stallion Returns*. (It is believed Cloud died in 2016.) In addition to horses, the Pryor Mountain Wild Horse Range is also home to mule deer, black bears, bighorn sheep, and coyotes. *Mustang Center: 1106 Rd. 12, (307) 548-9453, pryormustangs.org. (307) 272-0364, www.pryorwild.com*

LOCAL LOWDOWN
DIANE GRANGER, Board Member of the Pryor Mountain Wild Mustang Center

Diane Granger and her late husband, Walter Granger Sr., moved from New Jersey to Lovell, Wyoming, in 1993. "We went from the most populated per capita area in the country to the least populated," Diane says. "[There were] too many people there. We had always wanted to move out west."

Today Diane is a board member of the Pryor Mountain Wild Mustang Center. She has 13 acres abutting Bureau of Land Management (BLM) land, a simple log cabin, and many animals, including four horses adopted from the Pryor Mountain herd, about fifteen cats "that just showed up," and four dogs. Until a couple of years ago, she also had a goat, Dolly, and a fifth dog. One day shortly before Wally died, he saw a goat and a puppy walk past their cabin. "'We're not keeping them,' he told me," Diane says. "The next day he was like, 'What are we going to name them?'" They came up with Dolly and Blaze. "Everything that comes here stays here," she says.

Q: *How'd you go from New Jersey to Animal Kingdom?*

DIANE GRANGER: When I was a kid I had a pinto pony named Patches. I loved all animals. Sometimes I prefer animals' company to people's company.

Q: *Of all the places in the West, how'd you settle on Lovell?*

DG: In the late 1970s, we looked around Colorado Springs and liked it. When we went back to look more seriously 5 years later, it had gotten so built up. We thought, "Why don't we try Wyoming?" The next trip we flew into Jackson, rented a car, and drove around the whole state. We came down over the mountains and into Lovell and it was perfect. That's when we bought our land.

Q: *Was adopting wild horses part of the plan from the beginning?*

DG: Yes. We built a barn so we'd be ready for them.

Q: *How do you go about buying a wild horse?*

DG: The BLM rounds them up and announces an auction. The year we were bidding, they rounded up forty-eight or something. They divide them up in holding pens by age and sex and you go and look at them. I went with my neighbor Jane. Charlotte, the horse I ended up buying, she looked at me and I was like, "I have to have that one." I got her for $350 and my husband picked out a little black one, Christy. We got her for $125. No one even bid on her.

COURTESY DIANE GRANGER, PRYOR MOUNTAIN

196

Q: *What do you do with them once you have them? Can you tame a wild horse?*

DG: It took a while. I'm not a cowboy. They are certainly different than a tame horse. I had some cowboys down the street train them a little for me. I eventually rode both of them. But I've been kicked, stepped on, bitten, and bucked off. It takes time and patience. And lots of love.

Q: *You've since adopted two more Pryor Mountain horses?*

DG: The center had adopted Kaibab and Liesl several years ago, but since Liesl is blind, she had problems in the field by the mustang center. She ran into a fence and got all chewed up. It was decided I should take them, so I built another barn and corral. They've adjusted quite well. Liesl knows her perimeters now and can run around. There's no way either would have made it out on the range. I even have to keep them separated from Charlotte and Christy. Mares especially will pick on something that is handicapped. They're doing really well in their own space though; Kaibab takes great care of Liesl. Now there are about 156 horses out there [in the range]. They're all named. I concentrate on the horses in the Dry Head area, which isn't up the mountain. I'm more comfortable going out in the bottom range. I could see one of these horses and tell you its name and how old it is.

There are about 55,000 so-called wild horses in the United States today, but given that their ancestors were domesticated, perhaps the better term for them would be "feral." North America was once home to truly wild horses, but they died out more than 10,000 years ago. Today's "wild" horses are descended from domesticated horses brought to the continent by Spanish explorers in the 1500s and 1600s. Genetic testing shows the Pryor Mountain horses are descendants of colonial Spanish horses brought to the area by Native American tribes in the 1600s and 1700s. Markings hint at this heritage too. All Pryor Mountain horses have a long dorsal stripe and nearly all of them have "zebra" stripes on their legs. These are considered "primitive" markings.

The only remaining species of truly wild horse in the world is the Przewalski's horse. These horses, which were down to a population of twelve in the 1960s, now number about 2,000. About 350 of them live wild on reserves on the Mongolian steppe. The rest are in zoos or privately owned.

GRANT ORDELHEIDE

YELLOWTAIL DAM

Yellowtail Dam was constructed over a period of 6 years in the 1960s. The structure that created the 71-mile-long Bighorn Lake is named after Robert Summers Yellowtail Sr., a Crow Indian. Yellowtail was born in 1889, and, at age 4, he was sent off to a boarding school where Native American kids were punished for practicing any part of their culture. After graduating from high school, Yellowtail studied at the Extension Law School in L.A. and eventually earned a law degree from the University of Chicago via a correspondence course. His goal was to be an advocate and protector of his tribe and their rights. His work helped American Indians earn the right to vote in 1924. While he won many battles, Yellowtail lost the fight against the dam, which would later bear his name. He was one of the fiercest opponents of the project because the Bighorn Canyon was sacred to the Crow. Yellowtail remained active in fighting for the rights of the Crow and Native Americans through the 1970s and 1980s. He died in 1988 at age 98.

Bighorn Canyon

To get to Bighorn Canyon, a steep, paved road runs through sagebrush flats to a parking lot near the canyon's rim. There's a lot of sagebrush there and little else for miles in every direction. At a signed viewpoint, the earth precipitously drops away 2,000-some feet. Way, way down below is a sinuous lake. Teddy Roosevelt had known about this canyon. He once came out here to visit Cedarvale Ranch, owned by his friend Grosvener "Doc" Barry.

Roosevelt's visit to this canyon preceded the construction of the Yellowtail Dam on the Bighorn River. The dam created a 71-mile lake, Bighorn Lake, which looks more like a wide, gnarled river because the canyon is so narrow. Its water ranges in color from navy to aquamarine.

About one-third of the Bighorn Canyon National Recreation Area (NRA) is in the Crow Indian Reservation. While permits are needed to access the reservation from the recreation area, the reservation welcomes visitors to the Crow Fair the third week of August each year. The fair, first started in 1918, is a celebration of Crow culture where tribal members erect as many as 1,500 tepees and visitors are welcome to learn about authentic Indian tribal traditions. *www.teepeecapital.com*

The Bighorn Canyon NRA was established in 1966, just as construction on the dam was wrapping up. Within the recreation area, there are four historic dude ranches (Cedarvale Ranch included), as well as 27 miles of hiking trails and marinas that rent motorboats and kayaks. You can also sign up for a scenic cruise. The road along the canyon's western rim is a gorgeous bike ride. *20 US 14, Lovell, (307) 548-5406, www.nps.gov/bica*

TRAIL TIDBITS

The Bad Pass Trail has been used for over 10,000 years, first by indigenous people, then, starting in the 1800s, by fur trappers, explorers, and miners. It is a sacred site for Native Americans and was added to the National Register of Historic Places in 1975. Most of the trail is no longer recognizable, and it is illegal to walk or drive along it. Three hundred cairns and as many as a thousand tipi rings remain though. The trail runs across the western side of Bighorn Canyon.

Along the Sullivan Knob's trail in the recreation area is a spot where you can stand on the canyon's rim and shout and get a triple echo in reply.

→ Chief Joseph Scenic Byway

Life in Wyoming can be tough. Take the Chief Joseph Scenic Byway (WY 296), one of the three scenic byways in this area. In most any other state, the Chief Joseph drive would be well known. Famous even. But in Wyoming, where there's the Beartooth Pass (page 76) and the Buffalo Bill Cody (page 151) scenic drives to compete with, it's often overlooked. Overlooking it is a mistake though.

The Chief Joseph Scenic Byway roughly follows the route its namesake took with 1,000 members of his Nez Perce tribe in 1877 as they headed for Canada and away from the chasing US Cavalry. It winds through the Two Dot Ranch, one of the oldest ranches in the area and once believed to be the largest ranch in the country. Today it's about 52,000 acres. You're not driving for long before you can see a series of switchbacks cut across the face of the red butte in front of you. After a 3,000-foot climb, you arrive at 8,060-foot-tall Dead Indian Pass, which protectively watches over one of the least visited bits of northern Wyoming, Sunlight Basin.

In Sunlight Basin are two hard-working rivers. Directly at the western base of Dead Indian Pass is Sunlight Creek, which, over its life, has carved a canyon between 200 and 300 feet deep. The Clarks Fork of the Yellowstone River is even more impressive. It is Wyoming's only Wild and Scenic designated river, and the gorge it has carved is as deep as 1,200 feet in places.

For the last miles of this scenic byway, it looks like you're headed straight into the Beartooth Mountains. Perfectly framed in the center of the view is the range's namesake peak, 12,351-foot Beartooth Mountain. The Crow Indians named this mountain *Na Piet Say*, which literally translated means "the bear's tooth." *scenic byways.inf*o

Combine this drive with Beartooth Pass. Starting with a turn onto WY 296, follow the road 46 miles to US 212, aka the Beartooth Highway. Take a left here and you go to Cooke City and Yellowstone's Northeast Entrance. Go right and you're on your way up to Beartooth Pass, heading toward Red Lodge, Montana.

The Chief Joseph Scenic Byway.
NICK COTE

←SUNLIGHT BASIN AND THE SUNLIGHT CREEK BRIDGE

Sunlight Basin was named by two early fur traders. Upon reaching the basin, which took significant physical exertion as they were there long before any road, the traders exclaimed something like, "the only thing that can get into this valley most of the year is sunlight." They're right. The west side of Dead Indian Pass is steeper than the east, and at the bottom is the canyon carved by Sunlight Creek. This canyon is so deep it takes nothing less than the state's highest bridge to span it. Built in 1986, the Sunlight Creek Bridge is 285 feet above the creek below. People joke the creek is wishfully named. Its canyon is so deep and the sides so steep that sunlight rarely reaches it.

Within a 100-mile radius from Yellowstone's West Entrance near West Yellowstone, Montana, you can find the seed potato capital of the world, the country's second-largest Superfund site (a hazardous waste site that the Environmental Protection Agency has identified for long-term remediation because of its impact on human health or the environment), one of the hippest mountain towns around, a 90-foot-tall statue of the Virgin Mary, dinosaur fossils, and the largest National Historic District in the country. The area surrounding the park's West Entrance is likely the most diverse. Some cities here pre-date Yellowstone's founding and they developed economies separate from the park. Missing cold-brew coffee made from single-origin beans? Head to Bozeman, Montana. If you're biking the Ashton-Tetonia Rail Trail, you'll see potato fields (and little else) stretching to the horizon. Even ghost towns have become vibrant destinations for travelers. In the 1860s, Nevada City and Virginia City sprung up along Alder Gulch after gold was discovered there. Today about 140 people live in the area and tens of thousands of people visit to experience life in a Victorian-era mining town. It's home to the Virginia City Players, the oldest continuously operating summer stock theater company west of the Mississippi.

Right off the interstate, Butte was one of the richest cities west of the Mississippi a century ago. Today its mining boom days are long gone and the city is decidedly depressed. But, what it lacks in polish, it makes up for with a downtown stacked with historic, brick buildings and an admirable originality. How many cities would think to turn a Superfund site into a tourist attraction and charge admission? Viewing it is worth every penny. Hang out in most of the cities or towns in this chapter and you'll feel millions of miles away from Yellowstone.

ROAD TRIP 1
BUTTE

For 16 years, I sped past Butte on the interstate. I hadn't heard many—or any—good things about it. Then in 2014, my boyfriend and I spent a long weekend there and we both fell in love. Montana and Wyoming are celebrated for their idyllic, natural beauty and cute small towns. Butte is a mining town gone bust with the country's second-largest Superfund site right on the edge of downtown. To write that Butte has rough edges is an understatement. But spend time here—eating a Cornish pasty, walking around the country's largest National Historic District, or hiking in mountains that offer views of both the Berkeley Pit (the Superfund site) and, in the distance, Yellowstone—and

tell me there's not beauty in the city's determinedly stubborn spirit, which goes back 150 years.

Our Lady of the Rockies

It's hard to miss: 90 feet tall, white, and perched at 8,510 feet on the eastern ridge of Saddle Rock Peak overlooking Butte. Our Lady of the Rockies is the tallest statue of the Virgin Mary in North America and the fourth tallest in the world. Behind the Statue of Liberty (305 feet) and a statue of Pegasus killing a dragon (100 feet tall and in Hallandale, Florida), it's the third tallest statue in the country.

Butte resident Bob O'Bill planned for a 5-foot statue of the Virgin Mary. In 1979, his wife, Joyce, was diagnosed with cancer, and, in a prayer, Bob promised the Virgin Mary he'd build a statue honoring her in his backyard if

Joyce recovered. Joyce did recover and Bob began to think a backyard statue wasn't enough.

From the backyard project, the statue grew to 120 feet high, but, per Federal Aviation Administration rules, anything over 90 feet tall needs an approved, blinking light on top of it. Not wanting to defile the Virgin with such a thing, the statue was shortened to 90 feet. If you think her head and arms look big compared to the rest of her, you're right. They were scaled for a 120-foot-tall statue and were not resized for the shorter version. Each hand is 8 feet long and weighs 300 pounds. The statue is made of steel and its separate pieces were welded together by Leroy Lee.

Bob, who died in summer 2016 at age 83, worked with friends and the Butte community to make the statue happen on a shoestring budget. Nearly everything was donated. Bake, pasty, and rummage sales helped fund what wasn't donated. Bob's friend Joe Roberts donated the land at the top of East Ridge. Four hundred tons of concrete were donated for the base. A Nevada Air National Guard team lifted and set the pieces of the statue into place with a CHAR Sikorsky Sky Crane—Defense Secretary Caspar Weinberger approved the mission, which was named "You Betcha Butte Mission."

Today a foundation maintains the statue and you can visit it during the summer and early fall. Buses leave from the Our Lady of the Rockies gift shop in the Butte Plaza Mall. *3100 Harrison Ave., (406) 782-1221, www.ourladyofthe rockies.org*

National Historic Landmark

Other National Historic Landmarks in the country are larger by area, but none contain as many artifacts—buildings and structures—as the Butte-Anaconda Historic District. In total, the district's 42.5 square miles have 6,013 historical artifacts in them. The area was designated a historic landmark not only for its significant copper production, but also for its role in the development of the country's labor movement. Butte is known both as "the richest hill on Earth" and also the "Gibraltar of Unionism."

As early as 1878, Butte miners created a union. The members of this union later went on to create the Western Federation of Miners, the Industrial Workers of the World, and the Congress of Industrial Organizations. It wasn't easy. Martial law was declared in Butte at least a dozen times. Local labor leader Frank Little was dragged from his house and lynched.

Between 1880 and 2000, the Butte Hill produced 22.8 billion pounds of copper, almost 5 million pounds of zinc, 45.3 million pounds of silver, and 187,000 pounds of gold. Between 1870 and 1983, over 2,500 men died in mining accidents, including a 1917 fire that choked off the Granite Mountain shaft, trapping and killing 168 men a half-mile underground. To this day, that incident remains the deadliest accident in US hard rock–mining history. The Granite Mountain Memorial honors the men who died in the fire, and also those who survived. The memorial is very well interpreted and a visit there is quite moving. Listening to voice actors read the letters of men who died—most died later of asphyxiation rather than in the actual fire—I cried. (If you can't make it to the memorial, the song "Rox in the Box" by the Decemberists is about the fire.)

By the 1890s, Butte was the largest city between the Mississippi River and the West Coast. Its population was almost 100,000 and there were sometimes 20,000 miners working in nearly 150 mines in the area. Recently, scientists at the Montana Bureau of Mines and Geology verified a Butte urban legend: 10,000 miles of mine shafts lay beneath the city.

LOCAL LOWDOWN

BOB MCMURRAY, **Owner of Old Butte Historical Adventures**

Bob McMurray didn't care about history when he moved to Butte with his wife in 1994. "But Butte history is so unique," he says. Now he runs Old Butte Historical Adventures, which helps restore historic sites and provides themed walking tours focused on different parts of the city's history—from its architecture and underground life to its former red-light district. *(406) 498-3424, www.buttetours.com*

Q: *What makes Butte's history so unique?*

BOB MCMURRAY: For decades, Butte was the center of power for Montana. Nothing happened in the state of Montana that didn't go through Butte. So many people think Butte was just a rough town, but it was also a metropolitan city back in its day. This combination of cosmopolitan city plus two-fisted drinking town is what makes it so special.

TORI PEGLAR

Q: Can you talk about Butte's cosmopolitan side?

BM: Butte had electrical lighting through the entire city in 1881. New York had electrical lighting in 1881, but the whole city didn't get it until 1886. There were New York architects working in Butte. Cass Gilbert built the Metals Bank Building in Butte and is famous for designing New York's Woolworth building and the US Supreme Court building.

Q: What about its two-fisted drinking side?

BM: In 2005, the Prohibition-era Rookwood Speakeasy was found in a boarded-up basement of a former hotel/boarding-house. Even if you had made it down to the basement, [the entrance to the speakeasy] was hidden behind a mirror in a coat closet. The original idea was that it was hard to find.

Q: What was it like when it was found?

BM: The woodwork and everything that is in there is all original. All we did was clean up and make some minor repairs in the ceilings. We didn't even paint in there. It's all the original paint. There's a hat, the gambling board, the red lamp sitting on top of the back bar. The floor is a 2.5-inch-thick, six-sided, hand-fitted terrazzo marble floor.

Q: Can people check this speakeasy out?

BM: Not on their own. We [visit] it on our Underground Tour.

Q: What are other places people can only see on a tour?

BM: The former jail where Evel Knievel spent a night. When the federal government shut it down in 1971, they classified it as a dungeon. There's another speakeasy too; hidden in a wall behind an underground barbershop. In 2009, I had a 93-year-old woman on the tour who, when she was a girl, was sent by her mom to find her dad at that barbershop. But she'd never found him there. She got very excited when I opened the hidden door. "Now I know where my dad was at!" she said.

Q: An underground barbershop?

BM: When it was a thriving city, Butte had blocks and blocks of businesses on a level below the streets.

Q: And did all of this underground stuff just disappear?

BM: As good as. The underground level was sealed off in 1968 when a flash fire ran through it. The city put steel panels over doors and windows and filled it all in with dirt. It was sealed until 2004 when some of the downtown sidewalks that had a level below them started falling in.

Q: How much stuff is hiding on this level?

BM: It's hard to say. There are sections all over downtown, but most are filled in. Between Broadway and Granite on one side of the street, probably maybe one-quarter of that distance is still intact underneath.

Q: What else is hiding around Butte?

BM: From my understanding, there were some buildings that burnt down years and years ago that shared a three-level sub-basement for parking cars. After the fire, supposedly they capped the basement off, with the cars still down there. Butte has all kinds of stories like this. If they were true and we could find these things, it would be totally amazing.

Evidence of Butte's diverse history can be seen in the mansions built by mine owners; the fourteen giant iron headframes, which stand directly above the old mine shafts and lowered miners, mules, and equipment as deep as 1 mile underground; crenellated brick buildings that were formerly banks and offices; and dozens of simple miner's houses. Many of the latter are covered in layers of soot and abandoned. Butte's population began to decline as copper prices fell after World War I and has stabilized at about 34,000. *Butte–Silver Bow Chamber of Commerce: 1000 George St., (800) 735-6814, www.buttecvb .com; National Historic District–butte-anacondanhld.blogspot.com/*

Copper King Mansion

It took construction workers and artisans 4 years to construct William A. Clark's thirty-four-room mansion in Uptown Butte. The Romanesque Revival Victorian home was ready in 1888. Other design features in the home include Tiffany stained glass windows, fresco-painted ceilings, hand-carved stair-cases and fireplaces (the bird's-eye maple fireplace in Clark's former bedroom is especially amazing), and parquet wood floors.

Clark made his fortune in banking before going on to own newspapers, a railroad, mines, smelters, an electric company, a sugar company, and oil wells. He also served one term as a US senator from Montana (1901–1907). The city of Las Vegas was built on ranchland he once owned in Nevada; Nevada's Clark County is named for him. Clark died in 1925. His last surviving child, Huguette Clark, died only in 2011, at the age of 104. She was a recluse with no kids and a $400 million fortune.

The Cote family has owned Copper King Mansion since 1953. Today they rent several rooms out as the Copper King Mansion Bed & Breakfast. Though Huguette never lived in her father's Butte home, one of the rooms available to rent is named for her and decorated in the style of a young woman. The mansion is open for guided tours daily from May 1 through September 30. (Tours are available by advance reservation other times of the year.) It was listed on the National Register of Historic Places in 1970. *219 W. Granite, (406) 782-7580, www.copperkingmansion.com*

Pasties

During its mining heyday, Butte was home to thousands of immigrants from Ireland, England, Italy, Wales, Lebanon, Canada, Finland, Austria, China, Mexico, and Croatia, among other countries. All of these cultures brought their own foods with them. Butte once had a bustling Chinatown stuffed with noodle parlors, but today the pasty—a savory pastry stuffed with meat, potatoes, and onions—of Cornish and Welsh immigrants is still going strong. It's the simple heartiness of a pasty that most closely identifies with Butte's character. At Joe's Pasty Shop, they use the same recipe that Joe Novack used when he opened in 1947.

Other miners saw the convenience of the Cornish and Welsh miners' lunches of meat pies and they caught on, albeit with some variations. Finnish miners stuffed their pasties with rutabaga.

Pasties are the size and weight of a brick, but it's still more difficult to pronounce "pasty" than it is to eat one. It's "PASS-tee" not "PASTE-tee." Joe's—and pretty much every other place around town that serves them—gives you the option of topping your pasty with gravy or not, but, since you don't need to worry about packing yours neatly in a lunch pail like miners did, it really isn't a choice: go for the gravy. *1641 Grand Ave., (406) 723-9071*

World Museum of Mining

The World Museum of Mining might be Montana's most interesting museum. You can travel in a steel cage 65 feet down into the earth, wander through a re-creation of an 1890s mining town in which buildings are stocked with thousands of period artifacts, admire a mineral collection with hundreds of specimens, and marvel at the level of detail in twenty dollhouses—all in the same visit!

Don't think that dollhouses and forty bisque porcelain dolls belong in a mining museum? The original owner of the collection, Samie Jane Keith, was a volunteer at the museum from its opening in 1963 until just before her death. In her will, she donated her collections to the museum. In addition to the buildings themselves, each house is stocked with hundreds of miniatures—look closely and you might see miniature cookbooks, dishes, and silverware. (A side note: At the time of her death in 2005, Samie was the longest continuous resident of nearby Ramsay; she moved there in 1937.) The oldest dollhouse in her collection dates from 1943. Some of them are modeled after real structures in Philipsburg, Montana.

The trip down 65 feet into the Orphan Girl Mine, a former working mine that is actually 2,700 feet deep, is as cool as you imagine. And it should not be attempted if you're claustrophobic.

Like the dollhouse collection, the museum's mineral display is the work of a Butte local, Roy Garrett. Roy's first mining job was in the Orphan Girl and he worked in the city's mines for 40 years. Among the specimens that come from around the world are copper, stibnite, malachite, and blue vitriol. The minerals in one display case glow under a black light. *155 Museum Way, (406) 723-7211, miningmuseum.org*

The Berkeley Pit

I've read that Butte's Berkeley Pit is "one of the only places in the world where you can pay to see toxic waste." I find it hard to believe that there's anywhere else in the world that has made toxic waste a tourist attraction. But that's part of what makes Butte awesome. It takes what it has and makes the best of it. For $2, you can access this Superfund site's viewing platform and peer down into the 1,780-foot-deep pit half-filled with water as acidic as lemon juice and laden with heavy metals like arsenic and sulfuric acid.

As crazy as this sounds, it's worth $2 to see the Berkeley Pit. Depending on the light, the "lake" looks like a bottomless black abyss or ruddy and red, with lime-green undertones. The red and green colors are from iron/manganese and copper in the water. The 700-acre lake is 1 mile by ½ mile; the sides of the pit are tiered and the range of colors in the different layers is beautiful—even reminiscent of the Grand Canyon—until you remember they're part of a Superfund site.

Active from 1955 until 1982, the Berkeley Pit produced enough copper to pave a four-lane highway 2 inches thick between Chicago and Long Island

The Berkeley Pit, a former open-pit copper mine, as seen from the viewing area in Butte, Montana.
TORI PEGLAR

(or a four-lane highway 4 inches thick between Butte and Provo, Utah). Silver and gold were also extracted. Scientists are now studying fungal and bacterial species that have evolved to live in the toxic water. Compounds isolated from the few organisms that can live in the pit have shown an ability to kill cancer cell lines.

Things in the pit's water might kill cancer; they definitely kill geese. A flock of snow geese landed on the lake in 1995 and overnighted on the water. More than 300 were found dead the next morning. That was the lake's deadliest night until 2016 when as many as 10,000 geese landed on the lake. The death toll release stated that "thousands died." After the 1995 incident, pit officials installed anti-goose technology, but it was all to no avail in 2016. The birds were unfazed by wailers, fireworks, and rifles fired in their direction. The pit's "Goosinator," a large, orange, remote-controlled boat meant to scare birds, was dispatched. The weather was so cold its batteries quickly died.

There is a federal law protecting migratory birds that allows for fines up to $5,000 for each dead bird. British Petroleum and Montana Resources now share responsibility for the pit. *300 Continental Dr., (406) 723-7060, pitwatch .org*

MARCUS DALY STATUE

Marcus Daly is the only one of Butte's three "Copper Kings" (Frederick Augustus Heinze and William A. Clark were the other two) to have been immortalized in a sculpture on display in the city. The Daly sculpture is also remarkable for being the last piece completed by artist Augustus Saint-Gaudens before his death in 1907. There are not many pieces of St. Gaudens's work in the West, but on the East Coast, he did the Sherman Monument in New York, the Adams Memorial in Washington, DC, and the Shaw Memorial in Boston. St. Gaudens also designed the $20 "double eagle" gold piece and the $10 "Indian Head" gold eagle. Daniel Hennessy, founder of the department store chain Hennessy's, which Daly was a financial backer of, financed much of the Butte sculpture. The statue was initially on Main Street in front of the Federal Building, but was moved to its present location at the entrance to Montana Tech in 1941.

ROAD TRIP 2
BOZEMAN

Undeniably the hippest of any community around Yellowstone, Bozeman is a college town set at the edge of Animal Planet and populated by uber athletes who make scaling frozen waterfalls look easy. In Bozeman, you can get killer cold-brewed coffee, browse a museum affiliated with the Smithsonian, and hike to the top of a 10,000+-foot mountain all in the same day. Montanans who live outside of Bozeman call the city the "Bozone" and joke that it's "20 minutes from Montana." Everyone else calls it pretty much perfect.

LOCAL LOWDOWN

JOE JOSEPHSON, Ice Climber

Born in Big Timber, 60 miles east of Bozeman on the interstate, Joe Josephson has mostly lived in Bozeman since 1998. Before that, the talented and avid ice climber spent about a decade living and climbing in Calgary, putting up many first ascents during his time there.

Joe has had a couple of short stints living elsewhere in the Greater Yellowstone Ecosystem: in Livingston (page 49) and in a yurt in Kelly (page 93). He's had the greatest impact in Bozeman though. He's been the director of the Bozeman Ice Festival since 2006; authored the most comprehensive guidebook for ice climbing in the Greater Yellowstone Ecosystem (*Winter Dance*); founded the 501(c)(3) advocacy group Friends of Hyalite, of which he's still the executive director; has worked with ranchers in the Paradise Valley to make wildlife-friendly fences; and is a conservation coordinator for the Greater Yellowstone Coalition.

COURTESY BOZEMAN ICE CLIMBING FESTIVAL

Q: *You've lived in a couple different gateway communities to Yellowstone. How do they compare?*

JOE JOSEPHSON: I don't think I know others well enough to compare them, but I know they're all quirky in their own ways. I've also observed over the years that the idea of a gateway community has changed. When I was growing up, it was Gardiner, West Yellowstone, Cooke City, and that was about it. You kind of thought maybe Red Lodge, and maybe Cody and maybe Jackson, but not really. They weren't like the towns that were right at one of the park's gates. Now though, the idea of a gateway is much broader. I think it's fair to call Bozeman a gateway to Yellowstone now.

Q: *Have Bozeman and the other gateways you know changed?*

JJ: Bozeman has clearly had a facelift and looks completely different than it did 20 to 30 years ago. But West Yellowstone and Gardiner and even Livingston—to some degree they're pretty much the same. Same motels, and same signs, and lots of family-owned businesses. Lots of places selling the same trinkets. You go to Banff [in Alberta] where there are Gucci stores and world-class merchandising and here people hang T-shirts on metal hangers in their window. I think that kind of Montana family charm is unique and steadfast.

Q: *During your time living and climbing in Canada, you traveled to some of the far corners of the world on expeditions. How does Montana compare?*

JJ: I've been to some amazing places and the single most beautiful canyon in the world is up the East Rosebud drainage [in the Beartooth Mountains]. And it is my home. I spent every summer hiking up that drainage when I was a kid. My family has a cabin there that my great-grandfather built.

Q: *What made you decide to write a guidebook for climbers?*

JJ: I have a guidebook brain. I have an attention to detail that is not common and an ability to obsess over [details] that not many climbers do. I could probably have been a really good accountant. A lot of guidebooks focus on the climbing itself and how fun and cool it is, but neglect stuff like how to find the climb. I tell them how to get there from the car to the base of the route and how to get off the top of the route. I give them a notion of what to expect on the climb, and then let them have an adventure.

COURTESY G. ADAM RUTHER

Hyalite Canyon

Hyalite Canyon Recreation Area is the most heavily visited recreation area in Montana. Its proximity to Bozeman–15 miles south of town off South 19th Avenue–has little to do with its popularity, but people (and their dogs) mostly come to Hyalite because it's freaking gorgeous. There are 10,000-foot peaks, waterfalls, alpine lakes, and wildlife from eagles to moose and grizzly bears. In summer and fall, it's hikers, hunters, campers, mountain bikers, paddleboarders, and runners who play in Hyalite. In the winter, Hyalite Canyon is unique in the entire country for its reliable and concentrated collection of natural ice climbs; there are over 225 identified ice climbs and there are still areas waiting to be explored. Nowhere else in the United States has anything like it. There are also groomed Nordic skiing trails and backcountry alpine ski terrain accessible to those with the proper experience and equipment. But winter access to Hyalite is a relatively new thing, and only came about after locals fought for it.

Hyalite is accessed via a Forest Service road. Hyalite Reservoir is about 10 miles up this road. The road itself is about 13 miles long and dead-ends at a trailhead. Until 2007, to the dismay of ice climbers and backcountry and Nordic skiers, it was not plowed during the winter. Not that that stopped adventurers from driving it. "We used to call it the Hyalite Rodeo," says ice climber Joe Josephson. "It was a pain in the ass getting back there and chances were you'd get stuck on the way."

But in 2007, the Bridger Ski Foundation got permission to hold an event near the reservoir and obtained a permit to have the road plowed. "By mistake, the county plowed the road all the way to the end, where the ice-climbing trailhead is," Joe says. "The genie was out of the bottle after that. The next day was like a Hyalite love fest. Hundreds of people were up there and loving it. It was a whole new world." Since then, the road has been plowed every winter. The road has the distinction of being the only federal road in the country plowed purely for recreational access.

Hike to the top of 10,299-foot Hyalite Peak and you'll find incredible views at the top, and all along the way. The trail, which is 7 miles one way, passes ten waterfalls. The falls are almost beautiful enough to distract you from the work of climbing 3,300 feet to the peak's summit. But not quite. This trail definitely tests your fitness. *Follow Hyalite Canyon Road to the trailhead near the Palace Butte campground. The trail starts here.*

Montana is the only state in the Lower 48 that doesn't border a state that has a city of 1 million.

Shortly after the road started being regularly plowed, Joe had the idea to found a nonprofit advocacy group for the canyon. Friends of Hyalite was born. "We work to increase awareness of the area and have cleanup days twice a year," Joe says. "We pack out 4 to 7 tons of garbage each time." In addition to trails, rides, and climbing, there are three Forest Service camp-grounds in Hyalite Canyon. *www.hyalite.org*

The LARK

The building that is today the LARK was thrown up hastily on Bozeman's West Main Street in 1964 as one of the many motor lodges of the Imperial 400 chain. In the 1980s, when the Imperial 400 brand was dissolved, a pri-vate group bought the motel and ran it as the Imperial Inn. It slowly declined until it was closed for good in 2009. And then it sat vacant for 4 years.

In 2013, Bozeman-based ThinkTank Design Group, co-founded by Brian Caldwell and Erik Nelson, began the process of transforming the dingy, dilap-idated space into a decidedly non-dingy dilapidated space. The LARK, named after Montana's state bird, the meadowlark, opened in April 2015 as Mon-tana's first retro boutique motel.

"We wanted to basically look at adaptive reuse," says Brian. "We were history-wise, so we were looking to upcycle this vintage motor lodge into something that wasn't a detraction but a gateway into our downtown."

Caldwell and Nelson first met and became friends as architecture stu-dents at Montana State University. They worked with about 200 other locals to transform the space. A team of ten artists, including the former art director at the Museum of the Rockies, an art teacher at Bozeman Senior High School, and an oil painter who founded a furniture and art gallery in a former mill, ensured that each of the thirty-eight rooms is unique. When asked if he had a favorite room, Brian said, "I'd compare asking that to asking someone their favorite song. Typically, it's going to be associated with a mood or a certain aspect of the music they enjoy. I appreciate some rooms for my favorite info-graphic art piece or the barn door graphic, some I appreciate for the amount of space or light, some for their position in the building." Many visitors favor the map room for its collection of USGS maps and ceramicist Patrick Hoff-man's wood-fired ceramic forms that can be rearranged into different com-positions. Hoffman is an art teacher at Bozeman Senior High School. *122 W. Main St., (406) 624-3070, www.larkbozeman.com*

The LARK, named after Montana's state bird, the meadowlark, opened in April 2015 as Montana's first retro boutique motel.

...KE. CLIMB. SKI. WORK. GIVE BACK. ...VE. CREATE. BUY LOCAL. BE NICE.

LOCAL LOWDOWN

BRIAN CALDWELL, Architect and Principal of ThinkTank Design Group

"Like any good architecture student, I made a graph with ski resorts on the left and architecture programs on the right," says Brian Caldwell (left in the photo below), a native of Grand Rapids, Michigan. "Big Sky and Bozeman's architecture program came together." Caldwell moved to Montana in 1992 and never left. He and fellow Montana State architecture student Erik Nelson started ThinkTank Design immediately upon graduation and their partnership is still going strong.

ERIC SCHMIDT PHOTOGRAPHY, COURTESY THE LARK

Q: *How has Bozeman changed in the time you've lived here?*

BRIAN CALDWELL: When I moved here, Bozeman was in its first burst of attention after *A River Runs Through It* had made it nationally known. Bozeman started off as an agricultural community centered around ranch life and being a small college town, and it's been steadily growing with the university being the primary driver. It's changed quite a bit, most of it for the better. There are those who lament the past, but I think the future of Bozeman is on the up and up.

Q: *What hasn't changed?*

BC: Two million acres of Forest Service and state land being so easily accessible from town is the same.

Q: *Is there anything about the change and growth that worries you?*

BC: I think it's really important that Bozeman maintains its sense of place and character as a community. Everyone is afraid of becoming like Aspen and affordability is already a big deal. Bozeman already has a bad rap for being only 20 minutes away from Montana.

The Museum of the Rockies

Jack Horner was the curator of paleontology at the Museum of the Rockies (MOR) for 33 years. During his tenure, he was responsible for growing the museum's dinosaur collection into one of the biggest in the country. He also discovered the first evidence of parental care among dinosaurs and was a recipient of a MacArthur Fellowship "genius grant." Perhaps that is why Horner was the inspiration for Dr. Alan Grant's character in all of the *Jurassic Park* movies. There's no denying Horner is a big deal, but he's not the only interesting person associated with MOR. The other candidate: Dr. Caroline McGill.

Dr. McGill, working with history professor Dr. Merrill G. Burlingame, founded the Museum of the Rockies after she retired at age 76. But before founding MOR, Dr. McGill was a family physician in Butte.

MUSEUM OF THE ROCKIES

LOCAL LOWDOWN
SHAW THOMPSON, **Misco Mill Gallery**

Bozeman's Main Street is full of art galleries, but Misco Mill Gallery isn't one of them. This gallery is in northeast Bozeman, in a grain elevator built in 1933 and renovated by two brothers, Shaw and Nate Thompson, and their dad, Sam, starting in 2001. The gallery exhibits pieces by Shaw and Nate as well as a handful of other Montana artists. Shaw is in the gallery most days but recommends calling first if you're planning to stop by, "just in case I'm running out quick to do an errand," he says. His wood shop is in the grain elevator too. "We were looking to buy a live/work space, but this building was way more than we were envisioning," Shaw says. "We all spent a lot of time working on it. And it's still not finished." *700 N. Wallace Ave., [406] 586-6833, www.miscomill.com*

Q: *Is Bozeman an artsy town?*

SHAW THOMPSON: [Yes.] Especially our neighborhood, which is the old industrial area. We've got a really nice little coffee shop directly across the street, Treeline, and a good bakery, Wild Crumb, two doors down. There are always art shows in both.

Q: *What inspired you to create art for a living?*

ST: I've been into art since [I was] a kid. In college, I majored in painting and drawing, and I started making furniture. A friend of a friend asked me to build a desk for them. We had always been a hands-on family—my dad built houses before he went into the Army—and I got excited about the prospect

of building a desk. I built it in the backyard of the house I was renting. Since then, I've done furniture along with my painting.

Q: *How would you describe your artistic style?*

ST: I have a constant battle trying to loosen up and go more abstract. I keep getting pulled back to architectural paintings that are pretty linear, so I'm struggling with breaking free from that. A lot of my subjects for the last few years have been grain elevators. What we've done with ours has opened a lot of doors for people in the area—they see what they could do with one. I think they are beautiful structures. Beautiful proportions.

Q: *And what about your furniture?*

ST: I use a lot of reclaimed materials, but do it in a contemporary design. I try to keep it super, super clean and let the elements speak for themselves.

Q: *Your younger brother, Nate, is also an artist. Is Nate's style very different?*

ST: Truthfully, we have kind of the same style. He has a similar aesthetic.

Q: *You've been working as an artist in Bozeman for some time now. How has the art scene changed?*

ST: There is much more appreciation for contemporary lines and a modern style. That's almost becoming the norm now. In the beginning, it was all rustic furniture. I never did log furniture, but that's what was popular. I use more steel now.

Dr. McGill moved to Montana in 1911 at age 32 to work as a pathologist at Butte's Murray Hospital. At the time, Butte had 275 saloons, a large red-light district, and stabbings and gunfights were regular occurrences. Dr. McGill wrote to her family: "I'll tell you right now I am making the biggest fool mistake to go . . . but I'm going. Feels sort of funny to stand off and serenely watch myself commit suicide, [but] I'll just have to let her rip."

Dr. McGill was the first pathologist in Montana. She had earned a doctoral degree in anatomy and physiology from the University of Missouri, where she was the first woman to be granted a doctoral degree by that university. She paid her way through college by chopping firewood and teaching. She earned her first teaching degree when she was 17.

After 2 years in the pathologist position, Dr. McGill left Butte to attend medical school at Johns Hopkins. Two years later, she planned to return to Butte with her MD, after a short stop over in Rochester, Minnesota, where she worked with the Mayo brothers at their clinic.

Back in Butte, Dr. McGill opened her own clinic across from Murray Hospital. It was at this point that she began collecting the artifacts that inspired the founding of MOR. Many of the smaller items in her collection were given to her by patients as payment; knowing these patients didn't have the money to pay, Dr. McGill was fine with bartering. Dr. McGill assembled a

MUSEUM OF THE ROCKIES

significant collection of porcelain from the Chinese patients she treated. She also scoured Montana's secondhand stores for pioneer artifacts. A memo she wrote found after her death titled "things to put in the museum" included thoughts on why a Montana museum was so important: "Much is being lost or taken out of state by collectors," she wrote.

In 1956, the then–Montana State University president dedicated three World War II Quonset huts for McGill's museum. She slept on a cot in one of the huts while she organized and catalogued her collection, which she had donated to the university, for display. The first iteration of the MOR, which was actually called the McGill Museum, opened January 4, 1957. McGill was the museum's first curator and continued to work with the museum until her death in 1959 at her ranch, the 320 Ranch (read more about this on page 257), in the Gallatin Canyon.

In 1965, the name of the museum was changed to Museum of the Rockies to better reflect its expanding collections. Today the museum's collections include more than 300,000 objects that cover more than 500 million years of history. It is home to the largest collection of dinosaur remains in the United States, the largest Tyrannosaurus skull ever discovered, and a T. Rex thigh bone that contains soft-tissue remains. Its hands-on Martin Children's Discovery Center is based on science in Yellowstone and is geared toward infants through 8-year-olds. See a miniature version of the Old Faithful Inn, fish from Fishing Bridge, and get a geyser to erupt by using a pump. In 2005, it became an affiliate of the Smithsonian Institute. And we can thank Dr. McGill for getting it started. *600 W. Kagy Blvd., (406) 994-2251, museumoftherockies.org*

Rialto Theatre

The Rialto on Main Street opened as a post office in 1910. "Then it was a tobacco store, then a business college, and was then turned into an agricultural implements store. And then in 1923, it became a theater," says Brian Caldwell, an architect and principal at ThinkTank Design Group, which is bringing the Rialto back to life. It has been shuttered since 2005.

The extensive remodel brings a tapas restaurant to the second floor. "It overlooks Main Street with a glow of the historic Rialto sign that we're bringing back to life at the full scale of the original Rialto," Brian says. "It's a pretty cool tribute to our past." There are also spaces for community events and shows. *10 W. Main St.*

ROAD TRIP 3
TETON VALLEY TO
WEST YELLOWSTONE

It used to be that people stumbled upon Teton Valley, Idaho—which includes the towns of Victor, Driggs, and Tetonia—when they were either looking to get into potato farming or they couldn't afford to buy or rent in Jackson Hole. Nowadays, it's because Teton Valley (population around 10,000) is an eclectic, laid-back community of artists, entrepreneurs, ski bums, farmers, and even the occasional billionaire or two (not that you'd ever be able to pick the

OLD MURPHY

...UD DRIVE-IN THEATRE 208-354-2727
Driggs, Idaho

NICK COTE

latter out of a lineup). It just so happens to be surrounded by mountains and streams perfect for outdoor adventures of all sorts. Welcome to the quiet side of the Tetons, with some extra credit excursions between Teton Valley and the park's West Entrance at West Yellowstone, Montana.

The Spud

Drive-in movie theaters are rare in the 21st century. So when there's a drive-in that is overshadowed by something parked in front of it, that "something" must be pretty spectacular, right? Meet Old Murphy, a 1946 Chevy truck with a two-ton potato sculpture on the back. The potato is really a potato-shaped frame covered in concrete and painted to look like a potato. Old Murphy is parked in front of The Spud Drive-In, which is just south of Driggs. The drive-in opened in 1953 and is listed on the National Register of Historic Sites and the Idaho State Historic Registry.

In recent years, the fate of The Spud has been uncertain. It almost closed in 2011 when Hollywood studios made the switch from traditional film to digital. At the time, the manager of The Spud found a used digital projector for $33,000 and sold T-shirts—"Save The Spud"—and advertising on fences around the drive-in to afford it.

While the projector has been modernized, the drive-in's Snack Shack is wonderfully frozen in time. Vinyl records cover the ceiling. Walls are plastered in record covers. The floor is a black-and-white checker pattern. You'll want

NICK COTE

to order a Gladys Burger—on the menu since Gladys and Leo Davis ran the theater from 1967 to 1987—or Spud Buds, also known as Tater Tots. *2175 S. Hwy. 33, (208) 354-2727, www.spuddrivein.com*

Pendl's Bakery

When Martha Pendl opened Pendl's Bakery in 2003, she did so with a lifetime of training under her belt. She grew up in her father's *Konditoreien* (the German word for pastry shops), Poor Richard's, and then Pendl's Pastries. Fred Pendl, Martha's father, was born and raised in Kitzbuhel, Austria, and began his bakery apprenticeship at the age of 14. He went on to work in London, Holland, and Munich before coming to Sun Valley, Idaho, to run a *Konditorei*. Fred and his wife, Edith, arrived in Idaho in 1966. Poor Richard's Konditorei opened early the next year and was soon one of the town's most popular après ski spots. In 1979, Fred opened Pendl's Pastries, also in Sun Valley. Both pastry shops were staples of Martha's childhood. You can see a photo of a very young Martha helping out with cookies on the Pendl's Bakery website.

Today Martha uses some of her dad's recipes at her own bakery. There's fresh (and flaky) *linzer* torte (a wonderfully crumbly lattice-topped cake usually filled with nuts and jam), *zigeuner* (a rustic cinnamon-spiced walnut

NICK COTE

macaroon with its end dipped in semi-sweet dark chocolate), and *nussknacker* (a decadent, layered tower of roasted hazelnuts and almonds and praline crème atop a flaky butter cookie crust dipped in chocolate). Pair any one of these with the bakery's cozy atmosphere—barn-red siding, white-trimmed windows, a faded green tin roof, a bright, woody interior, a constantly cranking (at least in winter) wood-burning stove, and a garden (in summer)—and you can't go wrong. Bonus: The bakery is open Sunday, which is a rarity in this Mormon-dominated area. *40 Depot St., (208) 354-5623, pendlspastries.com*

Today craft beer lovers can't imagine life without growlers. Rumor has it that the modern-day growler was only born in 1989. It was invented by Otto Brothers Brewery, which is now Victor's Grand Teton Brewing Company. *430 Old Jackson Hwy., (888) 899-1656, grandtetonbrewing.com*

Rail-Trail

Much of the Ashton-Tetonia Trail parallels ID 32. But while the highway has significant ascents and descents, the trail doesn't. There's a 900-foot elevation difference between the two ends (downhill heading north; uphill heading south). This mild pitch makes sense since the trail is a repurposed train track.

The idea of turning decommissioned rail corridors into trails started in the Midwest in the 1960s, not that there was any grand plan. Once rail tracks were removed, people naturally began going for walks on the gentle routes. In the winter, people skied on them. Today there are more than 1,500 miles of rail-trails in the United States used annually by 100 million people. The Ashton-Tetonia Trail might be one of the most scenic rail-trails in the country.

The 10-foot-wide trail with a packed gravel surface winds through potato fields, small riparian areas, stands of aspen, and over three historic trestle bridges. The Teton Range towers in the background on this ride from Ashton to Tetonia. *Trail info: www.traillink.com/trail/ashton-tetonia-trail; bike rental: Fitzgerald's Bicycles, 20 Cedron Rd., Victor, (208) 787-2453, www.fitzgeralds bicycles.com*

Mesa Falls and Scenic Byway

"I visited Mesa Falls before it was anything," says Sue McKenna, who has worked for the US Forest Service at Mesa Falls since 1997. She moved from Chicago to Idaho in 1974, "the year Nixon resigned," she says. "I fell in love with all of it. It was all so different than anything I was used to. I had certainly never met a cowboy in my entire life."

McKenna says Mesa Falls was a hidden gem when she started working there. "Summer weekends now, we're jamming." She thinks this is great. "The falls are just so awesome and spectacular," she says. "There is a rainbow next to the falls every morning until about one in the afternoon when the sun's angle changes. Another thing that is so astonishing is that you can get so close to them with the walkway. It feels like you can reach out and touch them, although you can't. People tell us it's better than Yellowstone. I think they say that because we're not as crowded as Yellowstone and in Yellowstone you can't get as close."

While both falls are impressive, the ten-story Upper Mesa Falls steals the show. The falls are about 116 feet tall and 200 feet wide. These two waterfalls are the last big waterfalls on the Snake River unaffected by human influences. *The Mesa Falls Scenic Byway is between Ashton and Island Park, (208) 524-7500, www.fs.usda.gov*

LOCAL LOWDOWN

KIM KEELEY, Owner of Victor Emporium

Kim Keeley moved to Victor from Jackson in 1997. "I realized I could buy a house here for what I was paying in rent or build one," she says. Having been a fishing guide since 1991, Keeley was familiar with the Victor Emporium. "I'd meet clients there all the time," she says. But she never imagined she'd own the historic general store.

Life as a fishing guide eventually began to wear on her. Kim remembers waiting for a client at the Emporium one September "and complaining about how much my back hurt," to her friend and longtime owner of the Emporium, Bob Meyer. Meyer told Keeley the Emporium was for sale. "'Why don't you buy it?' he asked me," Keeley recalls. She talked to Kathryn Ferris, another longtime friend who had experience in retail, about a partnership. Ferris said "yes," and the pair began talking to banks. They couldn't get a loan though. "I told Bob we had no money and he had us put together a proposal and they ended up owner-financing us," Keeley says. "Otherwise there is no way we could have bought it. They took a big risk on us." That was in 2000.

Keeley and Harris still own the Emporium and are still friends.

In her guiding days, Keeley would get a milkshake almost every day—Victor Emporium is famous for its huckleberry shakes. When she was a regular, it was always huckleberry (there are a couple of dozen other flavors available),

unless raspberries were in season. "When they had fresh raspberries, I'd do a huckleberry/raspberry combo," she says.

These days, Keeley says, "Being around ice cream so much, I don't hork down a shake a day anymore. I only occasionally have a little."

VICTOR EMPORIUM

You can buy fishing tackle at Victor Emporium. And Patagonia jackets and base layers. And postcards, stickers, T-shirts, sunglasses, and sunscreen. But it's the Emporium's thick huckleberry milkshakes that bring the most people in the door. Every summer, the store goes through 400 gallons of huckleberries, all picked locally. "We don't even put an ad in the paper telling people we're buying huckleberries," says co-owner Kim Keeley. "The tradition was there before we bought the store." Keeley says people come to them. "We buy a gallon from some people, but there are people who dedicate 6 weeks of their summer to following the huckleberries around and come in with so much." For decades, people have tried to cultivate huckleberries, but no one's been successful. They only grow in the wild.

The single busiest day for huckleberry shakes is always the Fourth of July. "We've done 900 that day," Keeley says. "The average summer day is more like 400." Huckleberry is by far the number 1 flavor. "Chocolate is second and then we have the Muddy River and the TNT, which are both popular but way down the line from huckleberry."

Since Keeley and co-owner Kathryn Harris bought the store in 2000, they've added items including a selection of novelty stuff, which they ingeniously display on the wall by the shake counter, where, because every shake is made by hand, you usually end up waiting for several minutes.

"My favorite is the emergency underwear," Kim says. "It's practical and funny at the same time." *45 S. Main St., (208) 787-2221, www.facebook.com/VictorEmporium*

LOCAL LOWDOWN

BRADLY J. BONER, **Photographer**

"I'm a history buff, especially for the American West," says Brad Boner, a longtime Teton Valley resident. Boner is also the chief photographer for the *Jackson Hole News & Guide* and the photographer and author of the book *Yellowstone National Park: Through the Lens of Time*, which includes 104 photographs he took in the same locations where William Henry Jackson took his 107 iconic images during the 1871 Hayden Expedition to Yellowstone. Jackson's images are a large part of why Yellowstone was made a national park. "I wondered if someone had ever gone back to Yellowstone and re-created the photos of the scenes that Jackson had captured." Boner discovered that no one had. "I couldn't believe it," he says. "I took the project on myself."

Boner spent months researching the images Jackson had taken. "Surprisingly there was no published single volume of Jackson's photos," he says. He then spent three summers between 2011 and 2014 finding the exact spots Jackson had captured with his 8x10 plate-size camera and taking the same photos. "I went into it without expectations; I wanted to be as objective as possible," says Boner. "I would say that for the most part things are strikingly similar to how they looked in 1871. There are a few places where you can now see roads, bridges, or a little bit of development, but there were places where individual trees and rocks still sat in the same place as when Jackson photographed the scene in 1871. These places where minute details matched up, I'd kind of get goose bumps. You really felt like

you were looking right into the past." *Yellowstone National Park: Through the Lens of Time* is available in bookstores around the Greater Yellowstone Ecosystem and also on *amazon.com*.

Q: *What was the first of Jackson's photographs that you re-created?*

BRADLY BONER: It was in the Grand Canyon of Yellowstone. A view of the Lower Falls.

Q: *Do you remember how you felt starting out on this project?*

BB: I remember driving up to Yellowstone to start and being excited. I was embarking on this adventure and I had it in my head that I was going to do this and follow through.

Q: *Was there ever a time when you doubted your ability to finish?*

BB: It was frustrating when I realized it was going to take more time and effort than one summer to do it the way I wanted it to be done—I'm nit-picky and I was waiting sometimes in certain locations for the right light or conditions similar to Jackson's photos. I never thought about stopping.

Q: *Which images were the most difficult to re-create?*

BB: The ones up on the Mirror Plateau, at Mirror Lake. Mirror Lake is one of the most remote areas in the park. We were hiking without trails for a long time, and we got into areas that had burned in 1988 and had to hopscotch through dead lodgepole that were like giant matchsticks someone

had thrown down on the landscape. I did a 10-day canoe trip around Lake Yellowstone to re-photograph all of his lake images.

Q: *How has this project changed your photography?*

BB: This Yellowstone project is a little bit of an anomaly for me. I'm not a nature photographer or a landscape photographer. This project forced me into that part of photography. As a photojournalist, I capture the moment. I've been forced to slow down and take the scene into consideration. What

this place has done for my photography in general is that it's really challenged me to be a reflection of the community I cover. Everything about this area—the landscape, the wildlife, the people—is unique. I have a real sense of duty to make a true and accurate reflection of that community.

Q: *What's a great place to get a guaranteed great image of the Tetons?*

BB: That's easy. The drive up to Grand Targhee. You can't miss it, especially in the evening.

LOCAL LOWDOWN
MELISSA ALDER AND KELLI HART,
Owners of Freeheel and Wheel

Melissa Alder and Kelli Hart became friends their freshman year at the University of Montana in Missoula. "We lived near each other in the dorm," Melissa says. That was in the early 1990s. They stayed friends through college, both working in Kelli's parents' fly-fishing shop in West Yellowstone for a couple of summers. Melissa learned to Nordic ski. In 1996, the two opened Freeheel and Wheel, West Yellowstone's first shop that specialized in Nordic skiing gear. In the time since Freeheel and Wheel opened, West Yellowstone has become a world-class Nordic ski destination. "The advantage is that we get snow early and we keep snow for the entire winter," Melissa says.

West Yellowstone made it onto die-hard Nordic skiers' radar in the late 1970s, and it was in the 1980s that Rendezvous Ski Trails became a community trail system. In the early to mid-1980s, local Doug Edgerton began building equipment specific to grooming Nordic ski trails. Today his company, Yellowstone Track Systems, sells grooming equipment to Nordic ski areas around the world. It's still based in West Yellowstone, but Doug no longer paints the equipment on his living room floor, like he did in 1984. By the late 1980s, an annual low-key early-season gathering of Nordic racers from around the West, called Fall Camp, had become a must-do for serious racers. Today

Fall Camp, always held Thanksgiving weekend, is the Yellowstone Ski Festival. It draws 3,500 Nordic skiers from across the country.

Melissa, Kelli, and Freeheel and Wheel have been in West Yellowstone for much of this. "When we first opened, we were looked at as sort of a threat," Melissa says. In the 1990s, before there were rules about snowmobiling in Yellowstone National Park, snowmobiling ruled West Yellowstone. "The snowmobile crowd was reluctant to accept us. But over the course of time, people realized it wasn't our intention to convert snowmobilers into skiers." Within 5 years of Freeheel and Wheel opening, the West Yellowstone Chamber of Commerce hired a full-time staffer to promote and coordinate Nordic skiing and other "quiet" outdoor recreation opportunities (like running and biking). "The number of skiers has grown roughly 10 to 20 percent per year," Melissa says. And snowmobilers still have 400 miles of their own groomed trails in the area.

Nordic skiers aren't flocking to West Yellowstone only for its early and consistent snow, but for Rendezvous Trails's 35 kilometers of groomed trails. Doug is still the one who grooms them, at least when he's not working as chief of course preparation at an event like the 2002 Salt Lake Olympics. He has consulted on the grooming for Nordic events at every Olympics since 2002.

"The Rendezvous Trails are great for all levels of skiers," Melissa says. "We have Olympians who train on them and people from Florida who are 70 and have never skied before."

While "we love the winter," Melissa says, the shop turns into a bike center come summer. Long before she learned to Nordic ski, Melissa was a bike mechanic and raced mountain bikes. Freeheel and Wheel has a coffee bar inside the shop that's the same regardless of the season; espresso beans are locally roasted by Morning Glory Coffee & Tea. *33 Yellowstone Ave., (406) 646-7744, www.freeheelandwheel.com*

Moose Creek Ranch

"They're really cute as a bug," says Jeanette Beard, the manager of Moose Creek Ranch outside of Victor of the ranch's "glamping" cabins. "There are lots of people who want to camp but are tired from traveling, so they don't really want to camp." The solution: the ranch's five wood-sided cabin-tents. They don't have indoor plumbing, but each has a queen-size bed, battery-powered lanterns, and a woodstove. Moose Creek burbles by close enough for you to hear it. In the fall, you might hear a bugling elk too. If you don't even want to pretend to camp, Moose Creek Ranch also has regular cabins with private bathrooms. Wherever you stay, "the nice thing about the ranch is that it's only 1½ miles off the highway. We're the only thing on our road and it feels like you've gone 15 miles away from civilization," Jeanette says. "There's no highway noise and you walk out the front door and you can ride, hike, snowshoe—do everything active that the Tetons are known for." *2733 E. 10800 South, (208) 787-6078, www.moosecreekranch.com*

Notice the moose in Moose Creek near Driggs, Idaho.
TRAVELING OTTER VIA FLICKR

ROAD TRIP 4
THE WILLIAMSBURG OF THE WEST

In the 1860s, Nevada City and Virginia City were two of nine towns that sprang up along Alder Gulch after gold was discovered there. As quickly as the area boomed though, it busted. Virginia City's population peaked at around 10,000 residents in the mid-1860s, but by the 1880s, only 200 residents remained. Nevada City was down to less than fifty people. Today roughly 140 people live in the area and tens of thousands of people visit to experience life in a Victorian-era mining town. Between them, Virginia City and Nevada City have over 200 historic buildings that are an interactive open-air museum managed by the Montana Heritage Commission. The buildings include everything from a general mercantile to a vaudeville theater, arcade, and music hall. There's a shop that sells homemade ice cream, too.

Nevada City Music Hall

You wouldn't expect to find the biggest music organ in the world in a Montana ghost town. Yet, there it is sitting in the Nevada City Music Hall—an 89-key Gavioli fairground organ almost the size of a house. And it's just one of the pieces in what is possibly the largest public collection of automated music machines in North America. There are also three Wurlitzer band organs, a Wurlitzer theater organ, and a machine in which mechanical fingers play a real violin. And all of these work, if you've got the chance to make them play.

The Butte Piano Company was once the largest dealer of Seeburgs and Violanos outside of Chicago, so there were quite a few player pianos in the surrounding area. Charles Bovey, the son of the president of General Mills, began collecting player pianos in 1946, about 2 decades after they'd fallen out of fashion. By this time, the Butte Piano Company, like Butte itself, was in decline. When Charles began looking around Butte for automated music machines to add to his collection, most of what he found still worked, most likely because of Montana's lack of humidity.

Charles found a Seeburg-G player piano, with its two sets of organ pipes and a set of drums, at the Lime Quarry Inn, west of Anaconda. Then there was the Seeburg-J, with its dome made from stained glass designed to look like the US Capitol. That came from the Montana State Prison.

LOCAL LOWDOWN

BILL KOCH, Co-Manager of the Virginia City Players

Bill Koch has worked for the Virginia City Players off and on since 1985. He and his wife, Christina, most recently took over managing the company in 2012 and have a 20-year contract with the Montana Heritage Commission, which owns the Virginia City Opera House. The first hour of every show is a classic melodrama–Bill or Christina writes the script. After a short intermission, there's a 45-minute vaudeville act. "We perform a variety over the summer," Bill says. "We try to do a classic horror show, and then a full-blown fantasy or comedy during the month of July when all the kids are out of school and then we try a murder mystery. The vaudeville part changes every month."

Q: Do audiences seem to have a favorite?

BILL KOCH: It is the melodrama that usually gets them in the door. It's the vaudeville that sends them out with their butt cheeks flapping.

Q: Where do you get the actors?

BK: They come from everywhere! It's funny what a small theater world the western US is. Past actors send friends to us and people randomly call us asking how they can audition to be a Virginia City Player. I've had people come work for me from Bakersfield, California, New York, Houston, Alabama, and Los Angeles. The difficult part is that they all live in cabins here. You have to find people who are willing to live in a cabin in a camping situation.

Q: What's the community [in Virginia City] like when all the summer tourists leave?

BK: There's a community Christmas potluck and everybody sits around the Elks Club and eats dinner. Every year, I emcee the cakewalk that raises money for the fire department. There is something so peaceful about living here. Once you're considered a local, and that takes some time, the community will do anything for you.

The Virginia City Players is the oldest continuously operating summer stock theater company west of the Mississippi. Founded in 1948, it performs melodrama and vaudeville 6 days a week (dark Monday) in the Virginia City Opera House. *338 W. Wallace St., (800) 829-2969, www .virginiacityplayers.com*

The Gypsy Fortune Teller inside Virginia City's Gypsy Arcade might be the only one of its kind left in the world. What makes the gypsy so unique is that she speaks your fortune from a hidden record player. Zoltar, a similar machine made famous in the movie *Big*, dispenses cards and doesn't talk. The gypsy was made sometime around 1906. In 2006, illusionist David Copperfield, a collector of such machines, reportedly offered $2 million to the State of Montana for it. But it wasn't for sale. The state got the gypsy when it bought all of Charles and Sue Bovey's collections for $6.5 million in 1998.

The bulk of Charles's collection came from New York though. In 1958, Charles met the owner of the B.A.B. Organ Company, which had recently gone out of business. Charles bought the company's entire inventory, from the tools and equipment that would keep the machines operating to the 89-key, house-sized Gavioli. The Gavioli was built in Paris in 1895, and, aside from its size, it is also remarkable for its hand-carved art nouveau exterior. There were about a dozen other music machines.

With such a large-scale collection, Charles needed someplace to store and display them. Luckily, the man collected old buildings at about the same rate he collected automated music machines. He owned a fair number of buildings in Virginia City and Nevada City. His music machine collection had fit into the Bale of Hay Saloon until all of the B.A.B. pieces came along. Charles thought a building that was once the recreation hall for Yellowstone's Canyon Lodge would be perfect for the enlarged collection. But first the building, originally built in 1910, had to be moved to Nevada City and then restored. This building was moved in 1959, and the Nevada City Music Hall opened the following year. *(406) 843-5247, www.virginiacitymt.com*

Open Air Museum/History

Bill Fairweather went looking for a spot to picket his group's horses for the night. What he found instead was one of the richest gold deposits in North America. He made his discovery late in the afternoon on May 26, 1863; within a week, word had gotten out and hundreds of men had descended on Alder Gulch to pan for gold alongside Bill and the other five men in his discovery party.

Today this area has been partly preserved and partly re-created. There are about 200 historic buildings that re-create a first-generation mining town. And they're open for business: spend the night at the Nevada City Hotel; grab a Montana microbrew at the Bale of Hay Saloon; cut into a steak in the former Wells Fargo building; or browse local art in several historic buildings.

Less than a month after Fairweather's find, nine mining camps stretched down a 14-mile section of Alder Gulch. The whole area was called Fourteen Mile City. Verona was the nicest of these camps and at the midway point of the 14 miles. A group presented the newly elected judge of the Fairweather Mining District a charter proposing this be a new town named "Varina." Varina was the wife of Jefferson Davis, president of the Confederate States of America. The judge was a staunch Unionist though and opposed the name. On the charter, he crossed out "Varina" and wrote in "Virginia" instead. Virginia City was born.

TORI PEGLAR

At this time, Virginia City and its neighboring mining camps, including Nevada City, were in Idaho Territory. Within a year, Congress established the Territory of Montana. Nevada City and Virginia City were both in the running, alongside Bannack, to be the territorial capital. Virginia City won and quickly grew to be the largest city in the inland Northwest; the population of Alder Gulch was estimated to be between 8,000 and 10,000, with Virginia City being the hub.

There were many other Montana firsts for Virginia City. It was the location of the state's first newspaper (the *Montana Post*, August 1864); the territory's first public school opened here in 1866; the first company of the Montana National Guard was organized in 1885; and it was the first town in Montana to have camels (1865, used for freighting). Virginia City was also the first administrative site for Yellowstone National Park when it was founded in 1872.

And then, by 1875, it was all gone. The population of the gulch was down to less than 800 people. Worst of all? The title of territorial capital was transferred to Helena, which remains the state's capital today.

Dredge mining came to the gulch in 1898, and while it resulted in an additional $285 million (in today's value) of gold being found, it destroyed many of Nevada City's buildings. Most of the rest were demolished when the highway was built through the center of the town. By the 1950s, Cora and Alfred Finney were Nevada City's last residents. Nevada City's remaining original buildings exist because the Finneys saved them.

By that time though, Charles and Sue Bovey had discovered the area. The couple had a penchant for collecting on a big scale. They began purchasing buildings and property in Virginia City and Nevada City in the late 1940s. They were also buying up old buildings elsewhere in the state. They didn't bring these to Nevada City yet. In Great Falls, where they lived, the Boveys founded the "Old Town" exhibit at the county fairgrounds. But in 1959, the city needed that space and asked Charles and Sue to find somewhere else for their collection. One by one, the buildings were carefully dismantled and brought to Nevada City to re-create the look of the town as it was during the mining days. The last building was moved to Nevada City in 1978.

Fourteen of the buildings today in Nevada City are original to Nevada City, including the jail, the Fenner Barn, the Finney homestead, and the Star

---

Virginia City got telephone service in 1902, but the area didn't have cell service until 2010.

Bakery. Today's Nevada City Emporium is an 1880s-era building originally from Dillon, Montana. In the 1860s, the Nevada City Hotel building was a stage station near Twin Bridges.

Deciding that the buildings were not that interesting when empty, Charles and Sue began collecting artifacts to go in them. Together Virginia City and Nevada City contain over 1 million Old West artifacts, the largest collection outside of the Smithsonian. The state bought the Bovey collection in 1998 and today the Montana Heritage Commission runs it. Virginia City was designated a National Historic Landmark in 1961 and added to the National Register of Historic Places in 1966. And among all of this is a living community—a small one with about 130 people living in Virginia City year-round—but a living community nonetheless. *Virginia City is 14 miles west of Ennis, Montana, on MT 287; Nevada City is another 1.5 miles west, (800) 829-2969, www.virginia city.com*

Placer Mining

The massive mining operations around Butte were hardrock mining; miners dug shafts and tunnels into solid rock to find minerals in their ore form. While some gold was found there, it was mostly copper that came from Butte's mines. In Alder Gulch, placer mining extracted about $2.5 billion worth of gold (in today's value) between 1863 and 1922. This was one of the richest gold deposits in North America.

At the time gold was discovered here, panning was the most common form of placer mining, but there are other methods. Generally, placer mining is any type of mining where raw minerals are deposited in sand or gravel. Other types of placer mining include dredging, sluicing, and using a contraption called a rocker. Dredging started in Alder Gulch in 1898, and, at one time, the gulch was home to the world's largest dredge. Dredging stopped in 1937.

Thompson Hickman Museum

Attached to the Thompson Hickman County Library, the Thompson Hickman Museum is awesome. Included in its collection is a petrified cat last seen alive in 1868 and "found some years later by Mrs. Emslie." And that's not even the museum's star oddity. That honor goes to the mummified club foot of "Club Foot George" Lane. In 1864, Club Foot George was hanged by the Montana Vigilantes, a group of locals who had charged themselves with keeping the peace and sometimes did so overzealously. (During their reign, they hung an estimated forty-four people.) A group of 20th-century locals had heard rumors of Club Foot George's hanging the century prior and decided to dig up his supposed grave on Virginia City's Boot Hill to confirm. The proof of Club Foot George the group found was indisputable. Now the object is swaddled in burlap under a protective dome and can be shared with others thanks to its appearance on a postcard the museum sells. *220 Wallace St., (406) 843-5238, www.visitmt.com*

◆ ROAD TRIP 5
GALLATIN CANYON

You'll be amazed by the differences between the two routes—US 287 and US 191—that connect West Yellowstone and Bozeman. Know you can't go wrong with either. Also know that if there's any way you can make a loop out of driving both, you should. US 191 follows the Gallatin River so closely for most of its length you could make an easy cast from the car. Not into fishing? Depending on the season, there's alpine and Nordic skiing at Big Sky, white-water rafting, hiking, and mountain biking along the way, too.

Gallatin River

The movie *A River Runs Through It* won an Academy Award for cinematography. The most beautiful scenes in it were filmed on the Gallatin River, feet from US 191. The story the movie was based on actually has the Maclean brothers

Lewis and Clark named the Gallatin River after US treasury secretary Albert Gallatin. Gallatin was in the position from 1801 to 1814, making him the longest serving treasury secretary in US history. (He served under both Jefferson and Madison.) Gallatin, a native of Switzerland, also served as a representative, senator, and ambassador (first to France and then to Great Britain). After retiring from politics, he helped found the University of the City of New York, which later became New York University. At the time of Gallatin's death in 1849, he was the last living member of Jefferson's Cabinet.

fishing on the Blackfoot River by Missoula, but when the movie was made in the early 1990s, that river was too polluted. Aside from having to pose as another river, the Gallatin didn't have to fake anything else for Hollywood.

In some stretches of the 120-mile-long river, it's estimated there are 4,000 mature fish per mile. You'll also see plenty of kayakers and rafts. This river has some of the state's best white water and it's all condensed into one 10-mile(ish) section. If you go rafting through the Mad Mile, a mile-long section of continuous Class III and IV rapids, know that at the turn of the 20th century loggers working in the canyon rode the logs down the river to prevent them from jamming.

The headwaters of the Gallatin are at Gallatin Lake, at 9,500 feet in Yellowstone National Park. The Gallatin is one of the three rivers that meet at Three Forks, Montana, to form the Missouri River (the other two are the Madison and the Jefferson). *Montana Whitewater: 63960 Gallatin Rd., (800) 799-4465, www.montanawhitewater.com*

320 Ranch

There are dozens of guest ranches in the Greater Yellowstone Ecosystem. But only one can claim ties to one of the most interesting women in Montana's history: the 320 Guest Ranch.

Dr. Caroline McGill, Montana's first female pathologist, the state's first doctor (she practiced in Butte from 1916 to 1956), and one of the founders of Bozeman's Museum of the Rockies (read more about the museum on page 229) bought the 320 in 1936. She had first seen it from the back of a bobsled in 1911, shortly after she arrived in Montana from Missouri to take the job of pathologist at Butte's Murray Hospital. McGill loved the wilderness and once wrote, "To get out into God's mountains, whether to ride, walk, or just sit, will cure more ills than all the medicine or medical knowledge in existence." An avid hunter, rider, and angler, Dr. McGill was a charter member of the Montana Wilderness Association.

Caroline bought the 320 from Sam Wilson, who homesteaded the property in 1898. The Wilsons had run the property as a small guest ranch and Dr. McGill continued that tradition. There was room for about twenty guests. In 1938, she elevated it above other guest ranches in the Gallatin Canyon by bringing in a Cadillac engine to use as a power generator. Thanks to that, the 320 had power 10 years before the rest of the canyon.

Dr. McGill retired to the ranch in 1956 and lived there until her death in 1959. The last cabin she lived in is now used for employee housing. It is called the Christmas Cabin because the ranch crew that built it for her finished it just before Christmas in 1956. "She was getting older at that point and the ranch crew didn't like that she was walking so far to the dining room," says the 320's current general manager, John Richardson. "So they built her this cabin right next to the dining hall."

McGill's original cabin, the one she used from the 1930s until the Christmas Cabin was built, is still on the property and you can rent it for the night. "We've got some great old photos of Dr. McGill as well," John says. "There's one of her leading a trail ride out of the barn. She was a truly amazing woman. Even by today's standards, she'd be considered a pioneer."

After Dr. McGill's death, the Goodrich family, the 320's longtime caretakers, bought the ranch and managed it until 1987. Then the ranch's current owner, Dave Brask, bought it. "It's pretty special we've only had five owners since 1898," John says. The 320 is also pretty special for how it operates today. "We're the only true a la carte guest ranch that I know of," John says. Most guest ranches are all-inclusive and have a minimum stay of 3, 4, or 7 nights. At the 320, you can stay for just a night. Or you can just come to the ranch for dinner, a trail ride, or to look at the historic photos of Dr. McGill. The original Wilson homestead cabin is now part of the 320 Steakhouse. *205 Buffalo Horn Creek Rd., [406] 995-4283, www.320ranch.com*

COURTESY OF 320 RANCH

LOCAL LOWDOWN

BRITT IDE, Former Interim CEO of the Big Sky Chamber of Commerce

Britt Ide grew up as an Air Force brat, but "Montana was always my anchor," she says. "Montana is my happy place." Britt is a fifth generation Montanan. "My grandfather was the first mayor of Clyde Park. My mom graduated from Bozeman High." Britt's daughter was baptized as a baby at Soldiers Chapel, where Britt's mom and aunt both played the organ during summer Sunday services when they were in high school. Britt and her husband, Alex, lived in Montana in 1995 and 1996 and "have been trying to get back since then."

After living in Boise for the last 15 years, the Ides finally came home in 2015. Alex is the principal of Big Sky's Ophir School and Lone Peak High School. Britt has her own consulting firm, Ide Energy and Strategy, which does energy policy and sustainability, and she was the interim CEO of the Big Sky Chamber of Commerce. Their house is walking distance to Big Sky's movie theater. "We hear the creek from our house, and one summer a moose nursed her baby in our backyard," Britt says. *55 Lone Mountain Trail, Big Sky, [800] 943-4111, www.bigskychamber.com*

Q: *What's your ideal Big Sky summer day?*

BRITT IDE: You wake up and it's that wonderful cool mountain morning. Then you go for a long hike and it warms up, but it's not too hot and you see wildlife. Then you have a great dinner out on the patio and walk to a concert or show. We try not to take summer vacation because it is so gorgeous here.

Q: *Can you recommend any specific hikes?*

BI: Go up to Ousel Falls.

Q: *What about the perfect winter day?*

BI: Sun and fresh powder, so I'll be skiing on the mountain, or snowshoeing. If it's not fresh powder, I might go skate skiing, [or] take the dog outside.

Q: *Do you have a favorite season?*

BI: I love snow and winter, and fall is gorgeous, and summer is amazing. I just have problems with May. It's gray and rainy.

COURTESY BRITT IDE

Q: *Do you have a favorite restaurant in Big Sky?*

BI: As the chamber CEO, I'm not allowed to have a favorite. All of our restaurants are so good–definitely much more than you'd expect for a rural town.

Q: *What makes Big Sky special?*

BI: It's this neat small town but not at all typical. There is world-class art and people coming in from around the world. My kids have had classmates from Russia and Austria. But with all of this worldliness, Big Sky is very much authentically western and Montana. It is still small enough to be real. There's a culture of helping and welcoming that I haven't found in other places. I'm sure I don't know everyone, but I feel connected, especially with my chamber position.

Q: *Big Sky Resort is one of the biggest and best ski areas on the continent. Are there lots of ski bums around?*

BI: We have a reverse bell curve with our population. There are lots of young adults working as lifties or in service and also a high percentage of retirees. There's a low percentage of parents raising families. But a lot of the families that are here started out in Big Sky as ski bums and made their lives here.

DONNIE SEXTON

LONE PEAK TRAM

The top of Big Sky's Lone Peak Tram isn't exactly at the top of Lone Peak, but walking the final 16 feet to the peak's summit is worth it. From there, you can see three states, two national parks, and more mountain ranges than you can count. A popular Big Sky sticker pokes fun at Jackson Hole Mountain Resort, 120ish miles south (and a little east) as the crow flies: It says, "From here, we can see your Tetons." And on clear days, you really can see the Tetons. The tram is open in summer (hiking) and winter (skiing). You can take it to enjoy the views year-round. *50 Big Sky Resort Rd., (800) 548-4486, bigskyresort.com*

Sky Rim Trail

What is perhaps Yellowstone's most scenic alpine hike is barely inside the park, and the easiest way to get to it is not from inside Yellowstone. Meet the 20-mile Sky Rim Trail, which, for 7 miles, traverses an undulating ridge and is unlike any other trail in Yellowstone. Yes, you read "20 miles," so this is a hike for the extremely fit. The ridge, which stretches between Daly Pass and 9,888-foot-tall Big Horn Peak, is the northwestern boundary of Yellowstone. It is also part of the last bit of land added to the park in 1927, according to the book *Hiking Montana*. You'll pass metal stakes at regular intervals while walking the ridge delineating the park's boundary. The trail is 99 percent on the Yellowstone side. Once or twice, you'll deviate out of the park and into the Gallatin National Forest.

Start from the Daly Creek trailhead north of West Yellowstone. While the heart of this hike is a ridge, there are 6 to 7 miles of walking through forests and meadows at the beginning and end. About 3 miles in, the trail leaves the meadows and enters a forest. By this time, you'll have already climbed 1,000 feet. Once in the forest, it's about another 1,000 feet to Daly Pass. A warning: the author of *Hiking Montana* grades Daly Pass as a Category 1 climb and writes, "it seems you should be about as high up as you can get, but you aren't even close to the top." It does drag on.

But, once you reach Daly Pass, it's less than a mile to the ridge that gives this trail its name. At this two-way Sky Rim junction, 0.8 mile past the Daly Pass junction, pay attention. A Sky Rim Trail heads north into the Buffalo Horn area of the Gallatin National Forest in addition to the Sky Rim Trail that heads southeast and stays just inside Yellowstone. Take a right at this junction for the Yellowstone Sky Rim Trail.

Once you leave the Daly Creek meadows, there is no water available until mile 16 or so. Also know that, like most mountain ridges, this one offers little protection or escape from inclement weather. If thunderstorms are looming, do this hike another day.

Once on the ridge, the trail is not as obvious as it is in the forest, but, even in the one instance it completely disappears, there's little danger of getting lost. For most of its length, the ridge is no more than 200 feet wide. (In many instances, it's much narrower.) Stay on the ridge and you'll be fine.

As you traverse the ridge, there are half-a-dozen (or so) ups and downs. None of these are more than 400 feet, except the final one, which is 500 feet.

Traveling the ridge, you've got 360-degree views. You can see the Gallatin Range and the Absarokas. Look behind you and you can see the Sphinx in the Madison Range. Big Sky Resort's Lone Peak is way in the distance.

The final lump in the ridge is the toughest, because of its vert, its steepness, and its looseness. It is best ascended by hopping hummock to hum-mock. According to the author of *Hiking Montana*, this section is "the most precipitous section of designated trail in the park, but it's not dangerous." You can stop in a large grassy field at the top of this hillside, but the 0.3-mile trip to the actual summit of Big Horn Peak is very much worth the effort. Not only is the trail itself a feat of engineering and execution—it is carved out of the peak's crumbly, cliffy side—but from the summit, you get expansive views back on the ridge you just traversed.

To get back to your car without completely retracing your steps, return to the large grassy field 0.3 mile below the summit of Big Horn Peak. Then follow signs to descend into the Black Butte Creek drainage. After you've descended for about 6 miles, take the Black Butte Cutoff Trail to get you back to Daly Creek. You'll hit the trail you took in 2 miles from the trailhead parking lot. *The Daly Creek trailhead is off US 191, nearly 30 miles north of West Yellowstone. The trailhead is signed.*

ROAD TRIP 6
MADISON RIVER VALLEY

It's a conundrum for every Yellowstone visitor with a car: US 287 versus US 191. The former is through the Madison Valley. The latter cuts through the Gallatin Canyon. US 287 is longer, but the driving is easier. The scenery on the two roads could not be more different. The Madison Valley is western bucolic, with mountains looming in the distance and wading fishermen casting their lines in gentle riffles. The Gallatin Canyon has steep rock walls and fast water. Don't pick one of these routes or the other—drive both in one big loop.

GLORIA WADZINSKI

Norris Hot Springs

When the town of Norris was founded in 1865, it was miners who laid down the first fir planks directly over the hot springs bubbling out of the ground. Over 150 years later, little about the wood hot springs pool itself has changed, but you can now soak and listen to live music 3 nights a week year-round while enjoying an organic pizza or salad. If you order pizza in the summer, many of the ingredients probably grew in the on-site greenhouse. And you don't need to worry about your appetite being ruined by stinky sulfurous water; Norris's spring is very low in sulfur and doesn't smell at all.

The town's founder, Alexander Norris, left much of his land in the area, including the hot springs, to his family. For decades after Norris's death, they continued to ranch and mine here, but the hot springs wasn't a money-making venture. They built a tiny bathhouse and put a locked fence around the pool. The key was in the care of a small bar/hotel in town. Local families without running water were welcome to take the key and use the hot springs.

Of course, the key was eventually lost in the 1960s. After the key disappeared, locals and Montana State University students just hopped the fence.

Norris's modern history starts in 1972, when Doris and Mike Zankowski arrived in Montana from New Jersey. They bought the hot springs and surrounding 21 acres and quickly shook things up by charging admission ($5) and instituting a weekly nudie night. When Mike fell ill in the 1980s, Doris sold the hot springs, but continued to live on the land she and Mike owned.

LOCAL LOWDOWN

HOLLY HEINZMANN, Owner of Norris Hot Springs

Holly Heinzmann grew up in Carlyle, Illinois. "Five generations from both sides were from this town of 2,000," she says. "But I graduated college and went west." She soaked in her first hot spring–Fairmont Hot Springs, 15 miles west of Butte–in 1978. She was immediately enthralled. "To be warm, outside, in extreme cold. What a gift," she says. Holly lived in Montana for 5 years after college and did regular hot springs tours with friends. "I visited Norris several times in the late 1970s and early 1980s," she says. After Holly left Montana to follow her career path, "I would return every few years and take my own hot springs tour," she says. Wherever she lived, "I always had a map of Montana on the wall, and the hot springs guides at the ready." She bought Norris Hot Springs in 2004.

COURTESY NORRIS HOT SPRINGS

Q: When did you decide you needed to buy a hot spring?

HOLLY HEINZMANN: I have old friends in Montana that will say, "you always talked about owning a hot spring." But it was a dream–wouldn't it be great, wouldn't it be the coolest thing? But it wasn't a plan, or goal–it was just out there as a dream.

Q: How many hot springs did you look at before buying Norris?

HH: In 2003, [my partner and I] bought a camper van, sold the house, and stored everything. We traveled for 4 months in the West; we looked at a dozen or more hot springs. I was pretty sold on being in Montana. No–I was dead set on being in Montana. I made an offer on Norris, but the ineffable former owner, Doris from Norris, did not make it easy. We rented a great place in Bozeman and drove to Norris every week, to both sample and deal.

Q: Montana has tons of funky hot springs. What makes Norris unique?

HH: The wooden pool. I hope I've kept the unique spirit by adding food service that uses produce from our own organic garden and a music venue that plays right to the pool.

Q: How often do you soak?

HH: I soak almost every day in all but the summer season. I would soak in the summer too, it's just more difficult because we're open longer and there's less private time to do so.

Q: What's the history of live music at Norris?

HH: My then-partner Tom Murphy got the music started. He and I played in a bluegrass band when we lived in St. Louis. There we had a habit, but not a living, from having meals and music jams at our home. Part of our thinking in buying Norris was that this "hobby" would have a commercial application. We began playing under a little pop-up. I got too busy to play, but great players kept showing up and very quickly music became a regular feature. My longtime friend Joanne Gardner was involved in most of these early hijinks. She is still booking our music with amazing aplomb.

Q: Do you live on the property?

HH: Currently I live next door to the hot springs, in a single-wide still on its wheels. It was used by Doris's sister Grace until she died. It was not a dream come true—living in a trailer—but I got inspired by the renovation challenge. Now it couldn't be more comfortable, has some kind of view, and it sure is a great commute.

But the new owner wasn't the best fit for Norris, and Doris soon bought the springs back. Current owner Holly Heinzmann bought the springs in 2004. The water is 120 degrees when it comes out of the ground. In the summer, water is usually cooled to the high 90s. "When it's cold, the pool might get up to 103 or 103.5," Holly says. "We believe it's better to look to soakers rather than a thermometer. If folks are sitting up on the side, the pool is too hot. If they've got their chins in, it's too cool. We adjust accordingly."

"Doris from Norris" is now in her mid-80s, lives on the west end of the property, and soaks daily. *42 MT 84, (406) 685-3303, norrishotsprings.com*

Quake Lake

Today the only thing hinting at Quake Lake's violent birth is its name. Unless the wind is whipping down the Madison River Canyon, the lake, 180 feet deep and 6 miles long, is placid. Most of its banks are thick with ramrod straight pines. Quake Lake, which is downstream from Hebgen Lake, was formed by a landslide that resulted from a 7.3 magnitude earthquake. This earthquake, which scientists say was comparable to the 1906 San Francisco earthquake, happened just before midnight on August 17, 1959. It is estimated to have lasted 30 to 40 seconds. The 80 million tons of rock, dirt, and debris it shook loose from Sheep Mountain traveled at 100 miles per hour. It reached and dammed the Madison River in less than 1 minute. Amazingly, Hebgen Dam, which was built in 1917, held. Parts of the floor of Hebgen Lake itself dropped nearly 20 feet; three sections of highway running alongside it collapsed into the lake.

It took 1 month for Quake Lake to fill. During this time, the Army Corps of Engineers launched one of its largest mobilizations ever in the western United States. Before the new lake's rising water breached the landslide debris, the corps raced to dig a channel into it. They succeeded. The channel

LEWIS & CLARK CAVERNS STATE PARK

Explorers Meriwether Lewis and William Clark did travel within the boundaries of Lewis & Clark Caverns State Park, but they never set foot inside the limestone caverns, which are some of the largest known limestone caverns in the Northwest. President Theodore Roosevelt named these caves after the explorers, recognizing that it had been over 100 years since the men's expedition yet nothing in the National Park Service had been named for them. Roosevelt created Lewis & Clark Caverns National Monument the same day he created Grand Canyon National Monument. Of course, the Grand Canyon went on to become a national park, while Lewis & Clark Caverns went on to become Montana's first state park. Once these caverns became a Montana state park, the National Park System was again without anything named in honor of Lewis or Clark. This lasted until 1978 when the Lewis & Clark National Historic Trail was founded. *25 Lewis and Clark Caverns Rd., (406) 287-3541, stateparks.mt.gov/lewis-and-clark-caverns*

was 250 feet deep and 14 feet wide when, on September 10, 1959, the new lake's water level reached the bottom of it and began to flow through it. To be safe, the corps cut a second channel; this one is only 50 feet deep.

While this earthquake and landslide gave birth to a new lake, it killed twenty-eight people, many of whom were camped on the banks of the Madison River. The landslide was the largest in the northwestern United States since a 1925 one east of Kelly, Wyoming. The Kelly slide (read more about it on page 90) was 50 million tons of debris. Interestingly, both the Hebgen and Kelly slides were on mountains with the same name, Sheep Mountain. Also, while the Kelly slide did not kill anyone in 1925, in 1927 when the natural dam it created on the Gros Ventre River failed, another twenty-eight people died in a flash flood that obliterated much of the town of Kelly.

Earthquake Lake Visitor Center opened at the west end of the lake in 1967. In 2014, a 5-year remodel/expansion was finished. Part of the visitor center is built on debris from the landslide; it faces the mountainside that slid. *Earthquake Lake Visitor Center is at the west end of Quake Lake, 45 miles southeast of Ennis on US 287, (406) 682-7620, www.fs.usda.gov*

Willie's Distillery

"I can never go wrong with honey moonshine," says Robin Blazer, who founded Willie's Distillery on Ennis's Main Street with husband Willie in 2012. "It is diverse. In the winter, you can put it in hot water with honey and lemon. In the summer, you can mix it with lemonade and it is very refreshing. Or just put it on the rocks." In the distillery's tasting room, which is open 7 days a week, they make moonshine mules. "It's the best mule I've ever had," Robin says. You can do moonshine margaritas and Bloody Marys too. "It's really awesome," Robin says.

Robin and Willie didn't set out to start a craft distillery. Rather they first moved to Ennis and then started thinking about the type of business they could have that would allow them to live the lifestyle they wanted. "We settled on Ennis because it was close to family and we knew we wanted to raise our kids in a small town," Robin says. "We came here with the idea of a distillery and a dozen other ideas. I've always been a huge fan of really great tequila, not the shooter tequila," Robin says. "We started testing out whiskey, vodkas, and brandies and noticed there were some really, really high-quality liquors in the marketplace and knew that that was what we wanted to do, because that is where our tastes are—really high-quality stuff."

To start, the couple ordered a custom, hand-hammered copper pot still from Bavarian Holstein Stills in Germany. Then they set about finding the best ingredients they could. Fortunately, "Montana grows such high-quality

small grains," Robin says. "There's a place in Great Falls that provides malted barley to probably every single craft distillery in the country, or at least the ones that want the best." Robin and Willie were the company's first distillers, but eventually they hired Terry Barsness, who moved to Ennis from Minnesota for the job.

In addition to honey moonshine, which is made from three Montana grains and molasses, the distillery makes regular moonshine, bourbon, a Canadian whiskey, blackberry liquor, vodka, chokecherry liquor, and huckleberry sweet cream liquor. Some of the chokecherries used are from Robin and Willie's backyard. Willie's Distillery spirits are available around the Greater Yellowstone Ecosystem, but "there are some products we make you can only find at the tasting room in Ennis," Robin says. "We do really small batches of things for the tasting room." *312 E. Main St., (406) 682-4117, williesdistillery.com*

Ennis

Ennis is a ranching community with a fishing problem. It reveres trout. Proof: The town's welcome sign reads "840 people, 11,000,000 trout." And then there's all the fish art—along the Madison River, which winds through downtown; painted on the side of Montana Trout Stalkers Building (owner Joe Dilschneider commissioned the piece from Jackson Hole artist Abby

Paffrath); and set in the middle of the intersection of US 287 and MT 287. This intersection is the busiest in town but still I pay attention to Belgrade, Montana–based artist Jim Dolan's 10-foot-tall steel and iron sculpture of an angler casting his line instead of the traffic.

"I call Ennis the epicenter of trout fishing in Montana," says John Way, a fly-fishing guide and president of the Ennis Chamber of Commerce. "It's Trout Town, USA." John says it's often fishing that brings people here. "And then those people add to what's already an amazing community. You can't survive in Ennis unless you love being here and you love Ennis. The 900 of us that are here year-round love being here and there is a love for this valley and town that really shows. And we love showing off our town."

John says Ennis is "the perfect second western vacation." "Most people first come out west for a Yellowstone vacation. They want to stay in the park. But once you've done that madness, Ennis is the perfect second trip. It is close enough to Yellowstone to do day trips, but it's an actual town with great food and hotels and spirit."

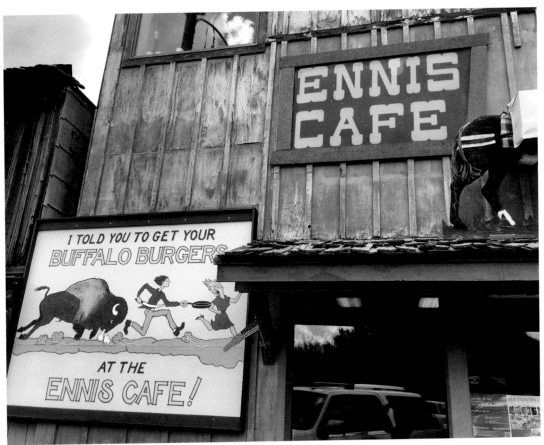

LOCAL LOWDOWN

JOHN WAY, Fly-Fishing Guide and Owner of The Tackle Shop

John Way grew up in the Catskill Mountains fishing the Delaware, Esopus, and Beaverkill Rivers. When it came time to apply to college, he swears he wasn't thinking about fishing. He picked the three schools with the country's top wildlife biology programs: Cornell, University of Montana, and Colorado State. He got into all three. Cornell seemed the obvious choice because it was closest to home and Ivy League. John went there for a visit. And "after that, there was no way I was going there. It just wasn't for me. I was a farm kid." It was only then that he started thinking about fishing. "If I was going to turn down the Ivy League, I wanted the school that had the best hunting and fishing," he says. That fall, John was enrolled at the University of Montana. "After a year here, I realized Montana was the place for me and that I was probably never going back east," he says.

John started guiding while still in college, and then after graduating with a degree in wildlife biology, he told himself, "I'm going to guide for as hard as I can for 2 years and then I'll go to grad school." Grad school never happened. Twenty years later, John still guides almost 140 days a year. He also now owns southwest Montana's oldest fly-fishing shop, The Tackle Shop. It was founded in 1937. *127 Main St., (406) 682-4263, www.thetackleshop.com*

Q: *You say Ennis is "Trout Town, USA." What makes the fishing here so special?*

JOHN WAY: The Madison is the big league. Everything else is AA ball. The Madison is on every fisherman's bucket list. It is the proving grounds for every fisherman in the world. I equate it to Yankee Stadium–the old one, before they built that new monstrosity. It's just got a magic to it. Everyone wants to see it and test themselves against it.

Q: *Why is the Madison so challenging?*

JW: I call it "random." It's just one big riffle its whole length. Most streams read like a book–there is a fish next to a rock, or next to a log. Here, because it's one big riffle, you have to look at the subtleties. You need a PhD in reading water to fish well here. You really have to up your game and read the water really, really well.

Q: *Are Madison River fish smart?*

JW: The Madison sees its fair share of pressure. The fish aren't spring creek smart, but they're not chumps.

COURTESY JOHN WAY, THE TACKLE SHOP

Q: *It sounds like it could be really frustrating. Should a beginner even attempt to fish the Madison?*

JW: Yes! We take new fishermen all the time. I'd recommend they go with a guide and, instead of making it solely focused on catching fish, make it solely focused on learning. In that 1 day with a guide, you'll learn a year's worth of experience in the school of hard knocks knowledge.

Q: *How much stock do you put into the history of The Tackle Shop?*

JW: It's iconic and I think about that every day. Here in the store above my desk, I have the names of all of the owners before me. I look at it every day and ask if I'm living up to the legacy of this place. The greatest thing is when I hear people that first came here with their grandfather and now they're in here with their own kids. Fishermen have been coming into these doors for 80 years. Literally. Right now, I'm struggling because all of the hardware is gone but I don't want to replace it. I want to keep the same door.

ACKNOWLEDGMENTS

NATIONAL PARK TRIPS MEDIA

As experts in national park travel, we started National Park Trips Media to make it easier for people to plan their dream vacations to national parks. From hiking along awe-inspiring trails, floating down beautiful rivers, and people-watching at historic lodges, we believe national parks and the attractions along the way truly offer something for everyone.

Every year, we help more than 6 million travelers plan a national park vacation of a lifetime. Our detailed trip-planning websites, *National Park Journal* magazine, park-specific trip planners, social media channels, and newsletters are packed with insider tips on what to do in and around the parks, including the best places to eat, sleep, and explore. We also have developed epic road trips with daily itineraries that highlight fascinating natural and cultural attractions and fun outdoor activities along the way.

Creating this book was pretty similar to one of our road trips. It was packed with anticipation, research, planning, and adventure. We'd like to

thank publisher Rob Wood and Lyons Press senior editor Holly Rubino for their vision in seeing this project as a vital guide for Yellowstone travelers and as an inspiring storybook for anyone who has traveled to Yellowstone and fallen in love with the vast natural and cultural ecosystems that surround the park. Rob also hit the road last summer with his camera, crisscrossing the park's East and South Entrances to take portraits of some of the incredible people profiled in this book.

Without our writer Dina Mishev, this book would still be just an idea. We want to extend a huge thank-you to Dina for her creativity, boundless curiosity, and powerful storytelling skills. She reveals the heart and souls of the communities that make up the Greater Yellowstone Ecosystem, inviting readers to be active travelers rather than passive tourists.

Digital producer Gloria Wadzinski offered crucial guidance and suggestions for this book, as well as conducted critical photo research to fill these pages. She also took a number of photos on her travels to and from Yellowstone that appear in here. Editor in chief Tori Peglar wrote and/or compiled the information that appears in the Yellowstone Primer section and worked with writer Dina Mishev and Lyons Press senior editor Holly Rubino on editing this book as it evolved from an outline to a robust insider's guide. She tracked down a number of the photographs in this book, taking a few herself while

driving the breathtaking roads leading to and from Yellowstone last summer. Photo intern Nikita Mamochine jumped in to assist, traveling in and around Grand Teton National Park last summer with a camera to photograph some of the area's iconic places and people for this book.

We are extremely grateful to talented professional photographers Grant Ordelheide and Nick Cote whose stunning photographs fill this book. They bring to life the West in ways few can. We thank them for the enthusiasm they poured into this project and for their persistence in driving the extra mile (or 250) to get the best shots. Both traveled through rain, snow, and blue skies to capture the vibrant people and places that make the Yellowstone region one of the country's most fascinating.

Lastly, we work under the umbrella of Active Interest Media in Boulder, Colorado, and are thankful to the wonderful community of outdoor professionals and enthusiasts with whom we work with every day.

DINA MISHEV

If it weren't for Harrison Ford, I would have moved to Colorado or maybe Utah when I decided I wanted to spend my first year as a college graduate learning how to ski. But, since Indiana Jones lived in Jackson Hole at the time, and because Jackson Hole had a world-class ski resort, I moved to the northwest corner of Wyoming. Even though I'm long over my coed infatuation with Indiana Jones, he still gets a big thank-you for leading me to the amazing valley that has been my chosen home for 20 years and that has so shaped who I am today.

Before Indy though, were my parents, Beth and Boyan Mishev, who raised me to be the kind of independent, adventurous (sometimes much more so than they would like), confident, and brave woman who would move to a tiny town where she knew no one, but did know her favorite movie star lived there. I can't thank my mom and dad enough for all of their love and support and awesomeness, and also for giving me such an amazing brother. This was not always the case, but today Rob Mishev is one of the people I admire most in this world. He and his wife, Gaby, are the parents of my two nieces, Maggie and Lila. I created a few of the road trips in this book with the hope we could one day do them together.

The residents and communities in and around the Greater Yellowstone Ecosystem were as helpful in the writing of this book as they are interesting. Everyone who suggested someone for me to include, and everyone whom I included, gets a thank-you as big and as solid as the Tetons. Derek Stal gets a special thank-you for being my happiness magnifier.

INDEX

GRANT ORDELHEIDE

GRANT ORDELHEIDE

NOV - - 2018